Sunny Memories of an Indian Winter

BGT
Dunn

Sunny Memories

OF AN

Indian Winter

BY

SARA H. DUNN.

AUTHOR OF "THE WORLD'S HIGHWAY"

"Eastward and northward journeying. The horns
Of white Himâla look upon the place,
Which all the year is glad with blooms and girt
With groves made green."

—Light of Asia.

LONDON:
WALTER SCOTT, LIMITED
PATERNOSTER SQUARE
1898

TO MY HUSBAND.

CONTENTS.

ILLUSTRATIONS.

———◦•◦———

PREFACE.

———•◦•———

HAD Diderot's lines fallen in less pleasant places
than in the sunny land of his birth; had he lived
amid the keen winds and under the sombre skies
of northern England, his sweeping condemnation
of "the traveller" might possibly have been modi-
fied. He might have recognised that conditions
were possible under which he need neither be "a
man without principle" nor yet one "driven forth
by a natural restlessness in spite of himself."[1]
It is no spirit of unrest nor yet any genius of
ennui which urges men and women to seek for
themselves, after the brief sun of the northern
summer has departed, some land where his rays
may reach them unhindered by sad, austere clouds,
and where undimmed golden light may be found
in place of chill, grey fog. It is but following a
natural law, an animal instinct,—for even your
dog follows the patch of sunshine as it travels
across the carpet, whereon to curl himself,—but
not, surely, for that reason alone does it call for

[1] Diderot's *Thoughts on Art*, Hon. Mrs. L. Tollemache.

apology. The need may fairly be classed as one of the "uses of travel" which Mr. Emerson held to be a legitimate occasion. Nowhere, perhaps, is the survival of the fittest better exemplified than in an English north-country winter. The stalwartness of the race is a fair gauge of the soundness of the law. Only the "fit" can encounter with impunity the blasts of bitter, relentless winds which sweep the stern and beautiful old Border county for many months of each year; and the less robust among the natives who can command the leisure are indeed "driven forth in spite of themselves," without, it is contended, laying themselves open to any charge of cowardly self-indulgence, or being branded contumeliously as globe-trotters.

Much has been written about India, and by some masters of their craft, but the field is vast and the land one of many phases. Much remains yet to be written; and probably no two pair of eyes will view it with the same vision. As for the following pages, they claim but to be some records of one of the sunniest seasons of the writer's life, and are reminiscent of that "Indian winter," the retrospect of which is "writ large" and in letters of gold on the tablets of her memory. In a country where an atmosphere of beauty, natural and artistic, is all-pervading, which is the breath of the people's life, which looks out from their eyes and sees and knows only what is graceful and lovely, it should be a very insensate soul indeed who could sojourn there and not be compelled within the magic thrall. They who have seen and felt the East, the mystery of its antiquity, the passionate splendour of its colour, and the spaciousness of its being, both past and present, they, perhaps, alone can realise to the full the alluring grace and charm of beautiful, imperial India.

But in the participation of any great good an instinctive desire arises to share it with others. The following series of sketches, reprinted in their present form by the permission of the Editors of *The Month* and *The Gentleman's Magazine*, were written during a winter of leisurely journeying in the Empire. In them, slight and most inadequate though they be, the writer tries to convey some idea of the delights such a season brings—at least to those who travel with open eyes and with faculties alive to the impression of beautiful and perfect things. They may, it is hoped, help those who know little of India, and who wish to ensure for themselves a winter of sunshine,—a thing not to be done on the continent of Europe, —to realise how easy of attainment, even to those of slender purse, is a winter sojourn there (where you not only reap all the financial advantages of the depreciated rupee, but may travel the length and breadth of the land in "first-class" luxury at a penny a mile); what a wealth of beauty is to be found in its mountains, its rivers, and its jungles, what amazing feats of artistic architecture in the mysteries of its palaces, its temples, and its tombs, and what a fund of large kindness in the peoples of its shining shores.

SARA H. DUNN.

SUNNY MEMORIES OF AN INDIAN WINTER.

I.

A WEDDING AND A BURIAL.

A LEGEND exists that the Parsis—the "Jews of India," as they are called by reason of their ready aptitude for finance and commerce, and their amazing capacity for growing rich—are a remnant of the lost tribes, banished from Persia because they clung to their own ancient faith. And it is conceivable that such an idea might vulgarly obtain, possessing so emphatically as they do so many of the attributes and participating so largely in the intellectual gifts of the Chosen People. It is hard to understand the decadence—almost the extinction—of so virile a race; or why the scanty remnant, the 180,000 who have made Bombay the city of their adoption, should alone endure to tell the tale of their primeval greatness; a tale told in no uncertain note nor in sounding words only, but in the still vital energy, the intrepid grasp of enterprise, the calm, strong spirit of self-reliance of those sons and daughters of Iran. Ever in the front ranks in movements of advance, and shooting ahead of their environments in a curiously facile manner, it is easy to associate them in one's thoughts with that great impulse of a remote century which lifted their race from the dead weight of idolatry and the gross deva worship of the ancient Aryan religion, and turned their minds from Indra, Bel, Nabon, and the rest of the Magian pantheon to Ahura-Mazda, the One and All-Wise God; thus approximating to the Hebrew conception of the Deity.

"You cannot belong to both of them (that is, you cannot be worshippers of the one true God and of many gods at the same time),"[1] said the organ-voiced Zoroaster, the warrior-prophet of Shushan, that "great and deep thinker" through whose enlightened reason the Persians of his age were helped to a new and higher order. "Perform you the commandments which were pronounced by Mazda himself and have been given to mankind. For they are a nuisance and perdition to unbelievers, but prosperity to believers in the truth. They are the fountain of happiness."[2] Neither did

---

[1] Yasna (Darmestater).   [2] Yasaa.

he stop short at reforms of the religious and moral order, but with a keen vision for the needs of his age, he took hold of its civil institutions, and with a strenuous finger beckoned his people on the road to progress—as *he* saw it. Especially did he urge them to that initiatory step to a higher civilisation, the use of the ploughshare and the sickle, where only herds and pastures had been before,—to "hearken to the voice of nature and to cultivate the land."

Very fine and malleable material would Zoroaster, with "that little book" of his, the Avesta, find to work upon, if we may take the Parsi of to-day, with his sound capacity, his mental and physical vitality, his mobility and his genius for commerce — almost Semitic in its instinct — as a type of his indefinitely remote forbears of Iran. The grave, strong, responsible face and self-possessed gait would alone mark the Parsi apart from an Indian crowd even without the ugly head-gear — like a mitre of black patent leather—and the distinctive tunic of white linen beneath which is worn the indispensable *sadaro* or gauze shirt, and the *kusti*, a woollen cord of seventy-two strands, both possessing mystical significance and as sacred and essential to good Zoroastrians as his scapular is to a Dominican, or the cord of St. Francis to a Friar Minor.

And their women—refined and cultured—are as unrestricted in their comings and goings as were the women of England's last generation. In the cooler hours of the morning and evening they may be seen, reposeful and unself-conscious, going to and fro in their clinging white skirts and silken *saris* of every tone of delicate colour cunningly and daintily broidered, the most pictorial raiment which ever clad the form of woman, and which, to see, makes the wearer of "tailor-made" garments and Worth's "creations" feel diminished and abashed.

These are a few of the many outward signs which, trivial though they be, help to recall the great and pregnant past of the Parsi and cause one to marvel that a race of such vigour and virility should have come, numerically, so utterly to naught; and, possessing such vitality, how it is that this handful of a people remains only a handful. It is not for want of marrying and giving in marriage, for that is an ordinance of such continuous occurrence that a great hall, or palace it might justly be called, has been set apart for the daily Parsi weddings of high degree. To such a one we were bidden, which was appointed to take place at five o'clock, the yearned-for hour when Bombay begins to simmer down as much as it is capable of doing, and when bleached *memsahebs* and white-faced *chota-sahebs* and *missee-babas* appear to take what air is to be had on Malabar Hill.

A grave and stately "master of the ceremonies" received us at the entrance of the brilliantly illuminated enclosure wherein were gathered a vast multitude of Parsis in ceremonial white linen and mitre-like head-dress. They sat in closely packed rows, looking infinitely bored in spite of the native band, which was doing the best it knew to make the waiting time pass nimbly. Through this male throng we were piloted to the great hall beyond, where a company of ladies were seated, also in rows—or rather squares—leaving a central space where the sacred carpet was already spread, and upon which were two expectant-looking chairs facing one the other, and presently to be occupied by bride and bridegroom. At either side were small tables bearing trayfuls of rice and cocoanuts.

A fresh and radiant effect of colour was produced by this assemblage of dark-eyed, olive-tinted women draped in heliotrope, blue, grey, and sky-*green*. Like the Japanese, they seemed to have taken their hues from a cloudy northern sunset—all guiltless of aniline. The only hint of barbarism lay in their jewels, ancient, priceless (some of them), and beautiful, but—too many. These

beautiful little women were more jocund than
the men, and their tongues more fluent, being to
that manner born, I suppose. Just beyond the
carpet—upon which no unhallowed foot might
tread—I found myself between two gracious,
pictorial little beings, who, in excellent English,
shed what light they could on the complex forms
of their marriage rites. A band of girls meanwhile
chanted in Gujerati a chorus both characteristic
and sympathetic.

The bridegroom was occupied in receiving the
congratulations of his men guests, a cashmere
shawl, the distinctive garb of a bridegroom, thrown
over his arm. Presently he was led by his friends
to the mystic carpet. He carried a gigantic
bouquet, and the heavy wreath of perfumed
flowers which hung round his neck gave him
the air of a sacrificial creature being led to the
slaughter. He being placed in one of the chairs,
the bride came, wrapt in a white and gold *sari*,
looking tired and anxious, as brides mostly do.
She sat opposite to him, a white linen veil being
held between to screen one from the other. A
strip of twisted linen was girt round the two
chairs, binding them, as it were, together, and a
consecrated cord was also wound about the man
and woman, passing through their hands. If by
mischance either let it slip it was held to be of

ill omen. In this case all went well, and amid applause and hand-clapping the linen screen was withdrawn and the bride's chair placed by the side of her husband's. Then began a homily in Persian delivered by the arch-priest, which, they not understanding,—Zend (ancient Persian) being the language of their prayer and sacred books,—was translated to them in a running accompaniment by the second priest. During the exhortation and the liturgical prayers which followed, each held in their laps a cocoanut, whilst the priests continually showered over them handfuls of rice—one being the symbol of plenty, the other of fertility. Presently the rice was thrown obliquely, and this, my little neighbour told me, was an indication that the ceremony was drawing to a close. Then the *saris* with one accord arose, and poured like an iridescent flood into the open quadrangle, where the banquet for five hundred guests was spread, and where the ladies—orientals though they were —were to be served first.

At their wedding feasts, Parsis use plantain leaves in place of plates and dishes. And very harmonious did it seem: those radiant little beings, like a company of brilliant butterflies of divers hues, each with her section of plantain leaf, about a foot square, spread on the table before her, upon which were small portions of sweetmeats, fruit, fritters, and poached egg. It was more like a feast prepared for birds than human creatures, and how they contrived to manipulate the eggs without aid of so much as a pair of chopsticks we did not wait to see. Probably very few tried. The quaint custom is part of their marriage formalities, which still receive very minute treatment in spite of the advancement of the people.

We left them as we found them, though the sun had not yet touched the horizon, in a blaze of artificial light. Devotion to fire and light, it would seem, was the singular feature of the ancient Magian worship retained by the Zoroastrians ; retained only as worship in a secondary sense and in as far as it was regarded as symbolic of the "inaccessible light," the All-Wise God. "The God who was seen and yet not seen, who was revealed every morning in the brightness of the dawn, and who Himself revealed, far away in the golden East, that infinite Beyond, for which human language has no name, human thought no form, but which the eye of faith perceives and after fashioning it into endless ideal shapes, and endowing it with all that is most beautiful in poetry, most choice in art, most sublime in philosophy, calls—God."[1]

[1] Max Müller, *Chips from a German Workshop*, vol. ii. p. 9.

And what more suggestive or significant figure could be found for Him than this "universal agent," the cleanser and purifier, the comforter and avenger, so benignant and yet so terrible, so beautiful to the infant eye of humanity in its lustrous red and gleaming gold? The races of earth's earliest æons were at one accord in their tendency to grant to fire a paramount importance in their religious worship; and the voice of the ages tells us that the divinities of nearly all ancient peoples were gods of light. What marvel indeed, when the lights and fires which hung in the limitless space above them were, perhaps, the only lights and fires they knew! We with blazing logs, glowing coal, and electric light among our common things may find it hard to realise what the earth must have been to its human occupants before the discovery of fire, and what the rising of the sun must have meant after dark, melancholy nights of danger, chill and dread. "Agni is awake," says the Veda; "out of the earth riseth the sun-god; Ushas the high yellow one hath dawned." What wonder that their wise men, with faces to the east and awe at heart, expectant and desirous, should wait only for the uprising of the Shining One, the turning of the golden tide, to prostrate with renewed joy and thankfulness! Was he not, so far as they knew, the giver of all

2

good things? "No incidents save of his causing, no delight save of his giving."[1]

Even from the standpoint of to-day, and in the clear light of Christianity, it is no hard thing to apprehend the spell which fire and light have cast over man from the earliest infancy of his race. Beasts, the most ferocious, feared it. Men worshipped it, because they were bound to worship *something*, and it was the most worshipful thing they knew. Surely the instinct was a beautiful and, relatively, a true one; a sort of foreshadowing of the heavenly vision of Patmos when the beloved of the Lord saw, burning before the Throne of the Ancient of Days, seven lamps—the seven spirits of God, an intuition of a completer knowledge, when that which had been the object of worship would become, not a figure only of high sanctity, as in Scripture angels are described as "wheels of fire, rivers of fire, burning flames," but a typical accessory to the service of the Christian Church.

Though we, in our nineteenth century wisdom, may be tempted, with something of levity, to smile at the childish souls who made gods of God's creations, we may do well to call to mind that even in *these* days of exact thought and higher criticism there are other meaner and subtler ways of stumbling into the same pitfall—ways

1 Mrs. Meynell, *Rhythm of Life.*

lacking the justification of simple ignorance and pure intention, and compared with which the fire-worship of the ancients was as light and life compared with death and darkness.

.　　.　　.　　.　　.　　.

In Parsi burials there is less of grace and poetry than in their weddings, but more perhaps of stern reason. The gruesome Towers of Silence, their "place of death," high up on Malabar Hill, are hidden away amid bowers of mango and palm-trees; beneath the trees are terraces of rose-beds under fringed and silken plantains, from which you may look down on Bombay in all the beauty of its domes and the green abundance of its gardens and boulevards. Look to the south-west and you will see its bay curving crescent-wise on one side to Colabar Point—stretching far into the Indian Ocean—and on the other to the wooded heights of Malabar; whilst its satellite isles sit, like outpost guards, round the beautiful harbour, in the still, purple waters of which great warships and stately white yachts lie motionless and idly dreaming, looking, against the crimson western sun, like "painted ships on a painted sea."

Of the five solemn, sombre, grey towers clustering among the trees like death in the midst of life, the ground plans are all on the lines of an ancient and mystical figure, that of Mazdayashnian Dakna,

or place of death, so vividly described by Mr.
Crawford in his *Zoroaster.* He tells how the
great Seer, when he made his sanctuary amid
the hill country of Chaldæa, traced this figure—
an intersected circle—on the desert plain, a thread
of strange mystic light following the tracery of
his finger; and that when he lay within those
lines of symbolised death he became as one dead,
his spirit, no longer bound by matter or space,
"being loosed in a trance and freed from the
bonds of earth," and thus rendered receptive of
the divine illuminations which were to aid him
in his reforms. This legend it is, and the firm
belief in it, which lends sacredness to the form
used in constructing the Silent Towers of the
Parsis.

Congregated upon the parapets of the Towers,
as closely as they could perch, we found hundreds
of grim vultures waiting, with cruel, unflinching,
unblinking eyes, for the next funeral. They did
not wait long. Even as we lingered among the
tall cypresses near the "House of Prayer" a
procession wound up the steep rock steps of the
pathway from below. The "carriers of the dead"
came first, and they were followed by a multitude
of white-robed Parsis. The bearded men, whose
office it is to carry the pitiful dead through the
heavy metal door in the side of the tower, place

it, according to age and sex, on the outer, middle,
or innermost circle of open metal work grooves
which cover the yawning space below. They,
except the vultures, are the only living beings
that ever enter that chamber of horrors. That
which they place there will in two hours have
become a skeleton, which, when bleached by that
great deodoriser the sun, will be cast into the
central well of the Tower, there in the course of
ages to moulder into dust, and so to be forgotten
and dissolved into its elements "in the trackless
and undiscoverable waste of past mortality."

Apart from sanitary reasons, the insistent
veneration for the elements which has entered
into and taken forcible possession of the Parsi
mind is a strenuous cause of this strange and
remotely ancient method of burial. Zoroastrians
will not pollute anything so sacred as fire, neither
will they defile God's earth by contact with a
dead body, which they hold to be a thing unclean
—so unclean that the "carriers of the dead" are
a class apart, the office descending from father to
son. And even they perform the task gloved, and
with the use of a tong-shaped implement avoid the
defilement which contact by touch would bring.
Before leaving the ground they purify themselves
and change their clothing in a chamber reserved
for the purpose.

Yet this shrinking horror of soulless humanity goes with an immense and pathetic reverence for the dead. You have but to rest for a while near the House of Prayer—chapel we should call it—to realise the loving fervour of the invocations which arise thence for the souls which have gone to the "Great Hereafter," prayers which are figured, in the ready grasp of the oriental imagination, by the spiral forms of adjacent cypresses, rising as they do flamelike and direct to heaven.

Not only do they pray for the dead, but they have belief, in some sense, in their bodily resurrection. A wide departure this from the Aryan doctrine of spiritual transmigration. This may readily be traced to Hebrew influence during the age of the Jewish captivity, and that blending of the Aryan and Semitic minds which gave birth to Zoroaster's religious system. For tradition tells how he, in the days of "the great King" Darius, sat at the feet of Daniel, the princely prophet and governor of the Hebrews in Babylon, and learnt of him that larger and nobler worship which was to lead him and his people so many steps further on the way to the full light and knowledge which they desired so consummately, to a clearer view of the All-Wise Power

"Which makes the darkness and the light,
And dwells not in the light alone."

II.

BIJAPUR OF THE ADIL SHAHS.

AN Indian night-journey by rail involves little fatigue. There is none of the cramped misery incidental to the American Pullman car, nor the asphyxiation which overtakes you in the *wagons-lits* of a *train de luxe.* Each compartment of a first-class carriage is in itself a small bedroom with roomy berths and well-appointed lavatory, and no exasperating official comes to inspect your tickets at unholy hours of the night or morning. Under such felicitous conditions we left Bombay on one December night and sped, by way of Poona, through the Ghauts. Whilst we slept the white light of the Indian moon had silently silvered their heights and vales, so that when, in a half-waking moment, we peered out of the window, it seemed as though a sheet of hoar frost had unaccountably veiled and transfigured the land.

At Hotge we changed from the G.I.P. on to a narrow gauge line, and thence progressed, through the yellow dawn of the Deccan, at the brisk rate of ten miles an hour, past villages of wretched mud huts, across flat and sunburnt plains that stretched away into the horizon like seas of rich-toned golds and browns merging into purple and grey distances.

Black deer raced and bounded alongside of the train, and gaunt-looking buffaloes, with their dusky herdsmen, were scattered here and there nibbling, and vainly searching if they might find, amid the ready-made hay of this parched and thirsty land, at least a few succulent green blades. Tracts of heavy-headed jowari, cotton, and wheat, carefully irrigated and vividly green, now and again refreshed the eye; so also did the clumps and hedges, heavily weighted with crimson fruit and waxen pink flower of the prickly pear, and the occasional groups of feathery tamarinds and yellow-blossomed baubul-trees. Except for these there could not have been the legions of birds, the pearl-grey doves, the green paroquets, the coal-black kingcrows, and the bee-birds that flitted and twitted and cooed in the morning light.

This picture hardly conveys an impression of beauty; and yet the sunlight and the colour, the glow of the atmosphere and of the sky, possessed in themselves an element of beauty singular and essential, not to speak of the beauty of Indian humanity. What a model for a painter, for instance, was that Canarese girl as she stood on the little raised platform in the midst of the jowari field! What foolish birds to fear such a beautiful scarecrow! There would seem little to terrify in that supple, graceful form, moulded on the lines of a young queen, the copper-bronze limbs partly draped in a rough nectarine-coloured *sari*. But in the folds of that *sari* there was a goodly store of sharp stones, and the small brown hands were very skilful in dealing death from the sling which they wielded to the feathered poachers of which she was the terror. Then again there were the pictorial groups of natives—men, women, and children, clothed and unclothed—waiting at each station, to whom the passing of the train is still the event of the day, and who, with their unpractical, mystical, incurious minds, never cease to marvel at the wonders of the steam-engine.

.   .   .   .   .   .

We saw Bijapur and its monster dome, looming mirage-like and in majestic isolation, for an hour before we reached it; for the ancient city sits solitary and desolate nearly on the crest of one of the great wave-traps of the Deccan, and in the

midst of the burnt-up arid desert which surrounds
it. It covers an immense area of mounds and
undulations interspersed with patches of scorched
turf. Quite a network of roads stretches over it,
some of which are those of the ancient city, notably
one three miles long which may still be traced, and
which was the principal thoroughfare in the time
of the Adil Shahs. Bijapur, the "city of victory,"
may best be described as a city of beautiful ruins.
Where there are no longer mosques and palaces
and mausoleums there are the remains of them,
mostly beautiful in their decay, and embedded,
as it were, in an all-embracing undergrowth and
thicket of prickly pear, at present a mass of bloom
and fruit intermingled.

There still exist the fort and its citadel. The
wall of enormous thickness, with the crenulated
battlements and broad fosse which enclose them,
is six miles in circumference. The great gateway,
with its flanking ramparts, is still there, so also
are the loop-holed towers and bastions fitted for
artillery. There are guns also which, in point of
size, might challenge most of those of the present
day. One especially, the "Lord of the Plains,"
which was cast in Ahmednugger in 1551, claimed,
until very recently, to be the largest piece of
ordnance in the world. Its circumference is
thirteen feet six inches, and the diameter of its

bore is more than two feet. Among the many other curious old field-pieces lying about Bijapur there is one on the top of the Haidar bastion called the Lamcharri or "Far Flier," which is constructed of longitudinal bars thirty feet in length, bound together with iron. So big guns were made in India before the days of Lord Armstrong.

The chief glory of the once royal capital is the Gol Gumbaz, the mausoleum of Muhammed Adil Shah, the last of his noble dynasty, which, for colossal majesty, boldness and breadth of conception, and simple, clear outline, is hard to rival. Measuring nearly two hundred feet square and of proportionate height, its material is rough stones covered with *shunam.*[1] On each of the four sides is a vast and lofty Saracenic arch filled in with solid masonry, the spandrils thus formed being embellished with very beautiful Byzantine ornament. Round the top runs a deep cornice of grey basalt richly carved and heavily bracketed, and supporting an arched and open gallery, above which again there is a crenulated parapet six feet in height, with gracefully wrought minarets rising from it at intervals. The dignified round towers at each corner of the tomb have seven storeys—each storey with

[1] A cement as durable as stone, and having the appearance of cream-coloured marble.

its eight arched windows—and are surmounted by graceful cupolas.

But the crowning triumph of this artistic work is achieved in its dome—the Rose Dome—which covers a larger domed space than does any other in existence, and in diameter lacks only fifteen feet of St. Peter's. The fashion in which the pendentives lead up from the square to the round is not only most skilful and graceful, but conveys the idea, even to an untrained eye, of an infinite stability and endurance. These, together with the majestic proportions and a sense of immense spaciousness, form the chief interior beauties of the tomb, which, like many of the holy places of the Mohammedans, is devoid of decoration. Just under the dome is the cenotaph, in white marble, of Muhammed, and at either side are those of his wives and his son. Over the entrance there are inscriptions telling of "Sultan Muhammed, inhabitant of Paradise," "Muhammed, whose end was commendable," and who "became a particle of Heaven" in 1067 (A.D. 1695).

The whole feeling of the place is suggestive of the tone of mind of the men who succeeded one another, during two centuries, in this, one of the noblest of the Indian dynasties. There is a breadth and grandeur of style, a simplicity and directness of aim, and a strength of purpose which speak

eloquently of the characteristics for which they—
taken in the abstract, and duly considering the
temper of those terrible times—were remarkable;
characteristics which embraced, among other fine
traits, a broad and tolerant spirit, exhibiting itself
not only in an impartial treatment of Hindus and
Mussulmans, but which was even extended to
Christian missions, many of which were endowed
by those large-minded Mohammedan sovereigns
of the Adil Shah dynasty.

The platform upon which stand the mausoleum
and its mosque is surrounded by a crenulated wall,
and in the centre is the tank running the entire
length of the mausoleum, thus separating it from
the mosque. In this mosque, immediately facing
the tomb, we have taken up our temporary residence, a corner of it having been apportioned by
Government for the use of travellers. There is a
piece of coarse bass matting stretched in the
travellers' corner, and there are some tables and
chairs, two bedsteads, and two wash-hand basins.
It is walled and partitioned to the height of nine
or ten feet, leaving the upper part of the arches
open to the outside, and except for spider-webs
and bird-droppings, is clean enough, though
certain holes at the junction of floor and wall
are somewhat suggestive of rats and snakes.
For your bath you must descend a flight of

stone steps to a cell below the level of the mosque.

The *khansaman* in charge, whom we take to be an old mess-sergeant of some native regiment, is a man with a joyless and somewhat scared countenance, giving one the impression that he had seen much sorrow and perhaps a ghost or two. He is, however, a person of much inventive genius, as is evidenced by the way in which he presents us, at meal after meal, with the same form of food under many subtle disguises. We have followed a box of sardines through a long and creditable career. First they were served *au naturel.* At dinner, the same day, boiled "fis" was an item in the bill of fare, through which the flavour of oil and sardine asserted itself. At breakfast on the following morning he tried to tempt us with "fis keks"—sardines again! And at tiffin that day the fragments that remained died the death in a curry. The buffalo butter of the country is of a blue-tinged white, and is far from inviting.

Oh, shade of Adil Shah! are you perchance hovering around us, tormented and aggrieved at your beautiful and holy place being defiled by the feet of the infidel? Good shade, I would fain make reparation to your sense of outrage if I did but know how. But we must eat and we must sleep. We can, however, undertake to abstain

from porcine flesh in any form during the brief
season that we must thrust ourselves upon your
sufferance — not that we are likely to have it
offered to us in this district of Mussulmans. And
truly the swine of the East, grey, lean, and unsightly, furnish a ready explanation of their
condemnation as unclean and unfit food for the
stomachs of followers of the Prophet.

Kassim, our sable retainer, whose duty it is to
make straight, as far as in him lies, the rough
places in our journeyings, had soon unfurled our
bundles of bedding, unpacked our deck chairs,
and lighted our travelling lamp. But at the best
it was an eerie place of lodging during the hours
of the night; and the sounds that came in from
the outer moonlit world were, to say the least,
startling to untutored ears. Not the least weird of
them was the eternal throbbing of the tom-toms
that came from a Hindu temple in an adjacent
grove. There was the howling of the jackals
which infest the thicket that spreads itself over
and among the buildings and ruins of the city;
there was the screeching of night birds, the
hooting of owls, the devilish laughter of a hyæna,
together with other wild and inexplicable sounds
which made one's blood curdle and sleep hard to
court.

Compensation came with the awakening. To

find oneself roofed in with fluted cupolas, round domes, and graceful pendentives, whilst the blue sky of the East looked in through the open arches over our partition walls—to see birds of divers sorts, whose homes are in and about the mosque, come wheeling and flying over our heads and even drinking from our tin basins,—made one almost question whether, after all, Aladdin and his lamp might not be something more than a nursery fable, and whether we might not, by some occult process, have been transported to the true and original land of Haroun al Raschid.

At breakfast, Kassim, with portentous countenance, asked solemnly, "Did *memsaheb* heard the ghost-woman last night?" At this *memsaheb* became fully alert, ghosts and snakes being the pet *bêtes noires* of her feminine soul. "Where was she, Kassim?" "On the steps of the tomb. No can see. Only hear. She scream." Though *memsaheb* could not honestly vouch for having heard *the* ghost-woman, she felt profoundly convinced that the nocturnal disturbances which she *had* heard were equal to any Walpurgis revels which had ever made night hideous. As for ghosts, their name in this country is legion. The folk-lore of Germany pales beside that of poetical, imaginative India. "There is not," says Meadows Taylor, "a rocky knoll, a quiet lake, a giant tree,

a broad river, or a secluded glen, which is not, in
the belief of the country folk, peopled by spirits,
nymphs, and fauns, or the scene of some stirring
event in their tradition." Every circumstance of
their lives, from their birth onwards, is compassed
about with religious forms, complex observances,
and superstitious fears and practices. Should a
man, on his way to work, meet a cat, or should
a snake cross his path, he turns back and makes
a fresh start later. If a blue jay is sitting on the
left of his road he will skirt round it so that it
may be passed on his right. Should a child,
through sickness, refuse the food which is proffered
to it, the mother throws some scraps of it to a dog
or a cat in the hope of transmitting with it the
child's malady to the animal. A few drops of
water sprinkled to the four quarters of the earth
and the murmured words, "May you live long," is
the pretty form of benediction with which a Hindu
woman of certain castes commences to bathe her
child. Sneezing is gravely portentous, according
to the number of sneezes more or less; and
whether the chirping of lizards is ominous of good
or evil depends on how often it is heard. Another
deeply-rooted superstition exists among the natives
concerning the pepul-tree—the *ficus religiosa*—
which they believe hears and understands all that
passes within its vicinity, and whispers to the

3

gods any offence committed against their code—
lying and cheating, for instance. And therefore do
they object to the tell-tale tree, with its emerald-
hearted foliage, being planted within the precincts
of the bazaar. "How can business be done with
a pepul always listening?"[1]

. . . . . .

Immediately outside of the Makka Gate is the
Ibrahim Roza, or tomb and mosque of Ibrahim II.,
the father of Muhammed. He was an artist and an
architect, and Bijapur owes many of its superbest
buildings to him. His mosque and mausoleum,
with the tank and fountain between them, raised
on an oblong platform in the centre of a great
courtyard, were not quite completed at the time
of his death, and were finished by his son Muhammed. Of about equal size, they are elaborate and
beautiful examples of Indianesque architecture.
Thirty-six years of time and £538,000, at the
present value of money, were expended over
them. If exuberance of ornament, of minarets
and cupolas, of deep and richly carved cornices,
of elaborately roofed arcades and heavy eaves, and
of an infinity of Byzantine decoration could satisfy,
then nothing is left to be desired. But they lack
the reserve and moderation of the Gol Gumbaz,
and thereby lose in repose and dignity. The eye

[1] Sir E. Arnold, *India Revisited.*

searches for rest and finds it not. I would rather
pitch my tent opposite the tomb of Muhammed
than over against that of his father. But to
wander among the old gardens and terraces—
now a mass of tangled creepers,—to peer curiously
about among the cloisters and outbuildings, to
find a cool corner on a massive stone stairway,
and there sit in the shadow of a mango or lime-
tree whilst green paroquets and small grey owls
call a council of war over the undue intrusion of
the *saheb loque* into their domain,—an afternoon
thus spent should be marked with a white stone
in the calendar of one's days.

Three weeks rather than three days could not
exhaust the wealth of superb Saracenic architecture
to be found in this city of decayed splendour and
glorious traditions. Our local guide is quite in
harmony with his environments—ragged, unkempt,
and never losing sight of his dignity. He pioneers
us solemnly through the complex network of roads
which have been almost hewn through the thicket
of prickly pears that held the ruined city in its
metallic embrace. From palace to mosque, from
tomb to citadel he leads us; to the Assur Shureef,
or "Palace of illustrious relics," standing now in
its original integrity with pillars of massive teak,
heavy porticoes, and tattered and faded remnants
of priceless carpets, even as it was built in the long-

ago palmy days of royal Bijapur, to be a shrine for the hairs of the Prophet's beard. Thence he takes us to the Jumma Musjid, where nine thousand good Mussulmans have knelt together in the midst of its vast cloisters and aisles ; and so on to the chaste and refined little Makka Musjid, a miniature mosque which lies like a gem in the heart of a monster compound. Enclosed with it are elephant stables and a great granary, and the fortress-like walls which shut them in have massive minarets at their angles. The delicate groined vaulting of the little mosque rests on slender graceful pillars, and it is built, like the rest of the city, of grey basalt, but in this singular instance the stone is highly polished, which accords well with the delicate proportions of the dainty building.

So we wander on, past roofless ruins which, in their day, might almost have been Gothic monasteries and churches; and climbing to the ramparts of the vast Pathan fortifications, or, better still, to the Palace of the Seven Storeys, the old-world home of an Indian " Fair Rosamund," from the third storey of the still noble ruin one may look out afar and, to the east, beyond undulating plains see naught but a shroud of golden mist. But there, we are told, flows the Dóne River of the Carnatic, which fills its broad valley with such abundance that the Mahrattas say of it, " If the crops on Dóne

River ripen, who can eat it? If it fail, who can
live?"

From the other side we look over the city, spread
out before us like a history of mediæval India. And
truly it is not hard to picture to oneself that things
are once again as they were; to see with one's mind's
eye the domes and minarets in their gilding and
many colours, the ramparts and towers in their
strength, and the palaces radiant and sparkling
in the jewel-like tiles and the delicately wrought
stucco which was creamier than marble; to see
terraced gardens—now dreary wastes—a wealth
of orange and palm-trees, of pomegranates and
champak blossom; to see the spray of fountains,
and to hear their drip and tinkle as they rise and
fall; to hear the *muezzin* chanting from this
minaret and that, in musical monotone, "La illa,
il Ulla," and to see the mosaic pavements thronged
with the faithful hurrying to answer his call to
evening prayer. There, too, is the Audience Hall,
where good Queen Chand of noble memory, with
her bodyguard of Abyssinians, held her durbars,
and ruled her people with the gentle hand of a
strong woman.

How unspeakably beautiful it must all have
been! And now a wilderness of ruins is all that
remains, and squalor has replaced splendour. The
fashion of Bijapur's mighty old world has passed;

but a wise Government has taken its mediæval
treasures into its own guardianship, and, with a
discretion unusual and very commendable, is pre-
serving them without attempting to restore them;
thereby earning for itself an unstinted measure of
gratitude from those who love and reverence the
matchless art of India.

III.

ROUND ABOUT A BUNGALOW.

EVERYTHING is relative, and after a residence of
no matter how short a time in a " rest-house," it is
humiliating to find how the comforts and luxuries
of a well-appointed bungalow appeal to one's
lower nature. Besides, this is an ideal bungalow,
with its spacious vestibule full of lounges and
books, and its cool twilighted drawing-rooms open-
ing, through a *tati*-hung arch, into the dining-room
beyond; its broad-eaved, flower-draped verandah,
from which a low bamboo trellise alone prevents
you stepping into the garden—a garden where
crotons and poinsettias, bignonias and caladiums,
palms and dracenas are contending for pre-eminence, where purple-winged stag-beetles hum and
red-throated lizards cheep, and which is an unfettered aviary of feathered beauty and sweet song.
Snakes, too, there may be, and doubtless are,
lurking around. Indeed, only the other day, when
the *memsaheb* was rising from her well-earned hour

of siesta, a snake crawled from under the very
cushion upon which her unsuspecting head had
been reposing. They are neither obtrusive nor
aggressive creatures, but the sense of this ubiquitous horror, this possible presence of evil under-
lying the fairest things in creation, is never wholly
absent.

The *memsaheb* of *this* bungalow is a very model
memsaheb. The effects of a tropical climate have
in no degree enervated *her.* When at 7 A.M., like
the valiant woman of King Solomon, she arises
and gives bread to her household—in other words,
dispenses *chota hazari* to her family and guests,
who assemble in the verandah for the purpose—
it is by no means her first appearance on the stage
of that day's play. She has already seen the
poultry fed, the Christmas turkeys gorged, and the
cow milked, a cake of "Sunlight" and a basin of
water having, to his great pain, been pressed on
the attention of the milkman before commencing
operations. She has inspected the daily instalment
of bread, the making of which, for the district, is
one of the prison industries, and the Madam
Saheb's basketful arrives with the dawn on the
head of a prisoner, a depressed-looking being in
prison dress, which consists of a large blanket,
through a hole in the centre of which protrudes
his shaven head.

After *chota hazari*, when the more trivially minded of the party disperse severally to take their golf, their riding, or their badminton, before the terrors of an Indian sun begin to make themselves felt, *memsaheb*, with the spirit of a Spartan, throws herself into the vortex of household duties. She reviews a small regiment of dusky domestic officials, telling off orders for the day to *wallahs* miscellaneous and innumerable. There is oil to see dispensed to the *mussaul* or "man of lamps"; gram (peas) to be measured out in her presence to the *ghora wallahs*, together with an injunction that it is meant for their horses' nourishment and not their own. (A very succulent curry may be made of gram.) The *pani wallah* is threatened with a "cut" when next month's wages are due for transgressing the laws of punctuality and causing domestic friction at tub-time. The day's mail is received from a *puttewallah*, whose mission it is to carry the letter-bag to and from the post, and to accompany *memsahebs* and *misseebabas* when they desire to go afoot beyond their own compound. Then occurs the opportunity of the *puttewallah*. Marching in front of his mistress and grasping a long staff, he waves it triumphantly before and around him, after the fashion of a band-sergeant, recklessly sweeping those of his own kind and colour from his path, and calling aloud to them in a tone of arrogance to get out of the way, as the Madam Saheb is coming. A more painful situation for a *memsaheb* of modest and retiring tendencies it is hard to conceive.

A suitable admonition has also been administered to the *hamál*, a majestic person in spotless raiment and ample turban, who dusts, and makes beds, but whose caste observances would on no account permit him to touch anything connected with cooking or serving food, and the meaner duties of whose office (of " housemaid ") are performed—tell it not in Gath—by the *mahatrani* or sweeper, whose name, so low is his caste and so degrading his work, must never be so much as heard in polite society. If, by chance, you cross the poor creature's path, he shrinks aside or vanishes like some guilty thing. His *salaam* would be regarded as an insolence and his touch as pollution, so impotent is Christian teaching in producing any sensible impression on the soul of this most immutable land. Nay, rather has the spirit of caste entered into and taken possession of the new administration.

In the *godown* or store-room *memsaheb* interviews Senor Geronimo Fernandez, whose historic patronymic would seem to convey the idea of some distinguished personage, but who is in fact her Goanese cook, an artist of some ability, who delights in displaying his powers on functional occasions, but who, in the privacy of a strictly domestic circle, is apt, sometimes, to overlook the interests of the family palate in those of his own pocket. His *ménus* are his crowning glory, though to the uninitiated some of their items doubtless call for interpretation. Who, for instance, could suspect that "solid roast pudding" indicated that dream-like *entre mets* "Charlotte Russe," or that " Poshekes anchy " could possibly stand for " Poached eggs on anchovy"? At times his dishes are so wrapt in mystery that one must needs accept them in blind faith, and with earnest hope that they may be less appalling than their names. As a rule, one's confidence is not misplaced.

Our own two sable servitors are Mussulmans of solemn and inscrutable countenance. The chief duties of the "bearer," a lordly soul who never forgets his dignity, and whose letters come addressed to Sheik Mahmoud Kassim, are to see that we never lift a finger to help ourselves and to keep his colleague the "boy" up to the mark. "Boys" vary in age from eighteen years to fifty, and why they are called boys no man knoweth. The suggestion has been thrown out that the term is derived from a corruption of *bhai* (brother). But, as the inimitable " Eha " points out, " The usual attitude of the Anglo-Indian towards his

domestics does not admit of that interpretation."[1]
Not that Indian servants have much cause to
complain of their treatment at the hands of their
saheb employers — at least among those of the
burra logue. Mrs. Flora Annie Steel, whose knowledge of Indian social framework—both European
and native—is so pre-eminent, told me that when
she first went out to India she asked a friend, who
had for a long period had her home in the Empire,
to give her any hints which might be useful to her
in the conduct of her life under its new conditions.
"My dear," said the old lady, "there are two
things I would have you observe. Be civil and
kind to your native servants, and stick to your
husband in 'hot weather.'" This lady was only
the representative of a class. Among the middle-
class Anglo-Indian officials there are doubtless
still "ladies" of the "Mrs. Drye Goodes" type,
who think it "good form" to treat their servants,
to speak to and of them, as though they
belonged to a different order of creation to themselves ; but it is a "form" which only brings
them into disrepute, and marks their own lack of
gentle breeding. In this matter nothing strikes a
traveller in India more than the fact that the
higher the social scale of the employers the more
scrupulously considerate and civil are they to their

[1] *Behind the Bungalow*, by Eha.

native subordinates. In India, as in England, masters and *mems* all have their characters as well as the servants, and very freely are they discussed "in bazaar" and at their clubs. Only those with good certificates get good servants; and not only are they good but devoted servants, who promptly place their masters on lofty pedestals, and to their greater social glory it becomes henceforth their highest ambition to minister. Not that they under-estimate the reflex of importance which is cast upon themselves. The very *dhobie* haughtily declines to wash the family linen with any but a *pucka saheb's dhobie*. He affably associates himself at the tank side with the washermen of the collector, the judge, and the parson, but there he draws the line. His dignity permits him to condescend no further.

By common consent the *ayah*, taken in the abstract, is pronounced to be the most difficult of the staff to keep well in hand. Separated as she necessarily is from her husband and children, and her domestic affections being thus more or less withered, a maternal instinct inspires her with an absorbing devotion to the *baba saheb* which is confided to her care, and which, if she had her own way, she would ruin by over-indulgence and unwholesome moral influence, worshipping the while. Her ministrations to grown-up *mems*

are not always so loyal, as the following incident
will show. Missee Baba, at the age of eighteen,
had rejoined her parents in India after a lengthened
sojourn "at home" for sanatory and educational
purposes. Thanks to a rich grandmamma, Missee
was possessed of many "contentments," as Indian
native ladies call them,—pearls, turquoises, and
sundry other precious vanities such as the soul of
a damsel loves,—and, girl-like, she had made haste
to display them on every available occasion. The
rooms of an Indian bungalow often open one into
the other in an inconsequent fashion, a *tati* or
bamboo fringe supplying the place of the open
door, privacy being subordinate to fresh air in
the estimate of the occupants. Missee's room
opened out of the dining-room, and a pleasant,
dainty room it was, spread with striped *dhurries*
and hung with Indian muslin.

On one Christmas night, after the neighbouring
saheb loque had been assisting her and her people
to make merry in approved British fashion by
discussing turkey and mince-pies, she was sleeping
the sleep of the just—so far as might be after an
orthodox Christmas dinner—in her little mosquito-
netted bed, a dim night light, according to Indian
custom, burning near her, when she awaked
suddenly and opened her sweet English blue eyes
to see standing by her side a lank black figure.

Its clothing consisted of the habitual loin-cloth and puggery. One end of the puggery was drawn mask-wise across the lower part of the face, leaving exposed a pair of gleaming eyes, which were fixed upon Missee with an unblenching and hypnotising gaze. In one hand he held a long knife. The girl was paralysed and speechless from fear, and though she knew that only a door separated her from her parents' room, she could not, even had she dared, cry out. Through the open doorway leading to the dining-room she saw through the *chic* two other dusky forms moving stealthily and noiselessly about by the light of a dark lantern, ransacking cupboards and drawers and stowing away into a sheet whatever commended itself to them as worth carrying off. They even squatted on the Persian carpet and regaled themselves on the fruit and wine which had been left on the sideboard, whilst the silent black image kept watch and guard over the poor girl who lay stricken dumb with horror. Then the two Dacoits came into her room, and going straight to the cabinet of carved *shesham* which held her treasures, they quickly rifled it of its contents, locked though it was. This was past feminine endurance, and she gave a little gasp, when in an instant a black hand was pressed upon her mouth and the knife lifted. Then she fainted.

In the grey dawn of the early morning her parents were aroused by Missee Baba, tearful, hysterical, and incoherent. The story which she managed to pour by driblets into their horrified ears might have been laid at the door of plum-pudding except for the disappearance of the family plate, some of the larger pieces of which were found concealed in an adjacent thicket, and her own pretty things. The cruel robbery was traced to the *malee*, whose bouquets and blandishments the *ayah* had found irresistible, and to whom she had confided all he wished to know. But such things are of rare occurrence among native servants, and, after all, such domestic treachery happens sometimes nearer home than in India.

. . . . .

A first Christmas Day in the tropics is a fact hard to realise. A bullock dumny, like a small tent on wheels, with ample canvas cover to protect us from the sun, carried us to church at seven o'clock. The dumny driver, sitting with his whip-hand lifted in mid-air, ready to bring it down in chastisement if need be, continually jerked it menacingly upwards as though the high-humped, cream-coloured bullocks had eyes where-with to see in the backs of their heads. To judge from the utterances which fell from him on this Christmas morning, he was not moved with that

universal sentiment of peace and goodwill which
the occasion demanded.   He cursed strongly in
Canarese, not only the *bhyl* that were trotting
briskly enough along before him, but their grand-
mothers and great-grandmothers, even to the third
and fourth generation of their female ancestry.   I
cannot suppose he meant to bring woe upon them,
any more than he meant to bring down his heavy
lash on their glossy hides every time he gave it
the threatening jerk.   It was merely a matter of
form.

And then the church—what an upheaval of all
one's cherished sentiments and memories!   In the
place of the beloved holly and ivy the little
building was a very bower of bougainvillier and
bignonia.   Instead of furs and plaids there were pink
and white muslin gowns and sun-hats, and in the
place of rosy, frost-kissed cheeks there were pallid
and sun-bleached ones.   The crib alone was the
outward indication of the great feast.   And so we
had to look below the surface to find Christmas,
with all its joys, hopes, and sorrows.   The congre-
gation was largely composed of natives; and very
pathetic was it to see the Indian women in
tinkling anklets and bangles, and wrapt in their
saris, bring their wondering brown babies to see
and kneel before the crib, and to learn from it the
" sweet story of old " which it tells year by year in

4

east and west, under sunshine and snowstorm, to
white man and black, to saheb and native.

.   .   .   .   .   .

This jungle district is a paradise of sportsmen,
because it is the home of game both big and small.
Tigers and panthers are to be found in the thickly
wooded hills and valleys that undulate over leagues
of the surrounding land.   Leopard cats and chetahs
lurk there also, as well as hyænas, wolves, and
bison.   There are savanur too, and wild dogs,
like the pariah dog, but with red coarse hair and
bushy black tails—a "cross" between a pariah and
a fox.   To go for an early morning drive into
the jungle with Madam Saheb is full of thrilling
incident.   "There," she will tell you, pointing to
a dense thicket in a sweeping hollow below the
ridge along which you are slowly driving, "is the
clump of trees, in one of which Mrs. B——, the
lady whom you heard receiving congratulations
in the club on having got a bison yesterday, sat
for the greater part of last Tuesday night with a
decoy kid tethered below her in hopes of luring
within range of her rifle a tiger, which was known
to be thereabouts."   "And here," as we cross a
railway track, "is the spot where Mr. S. a day or
two ago went to drive what he took to be a large
dog from off the line, across which it lay sleeping.
As he approached, the creature—a panther—got

up, stretched itself, and lazily lounged into the
jungle. Fortunately for him, it being Sunday, his
gun had been left at home."

With these and such-like anecdotes she inter-
sperses her conversation, whilst patient old Bhudda,
in the back seat, holds aloft, with an untiring arm,
an immense white umbrella between us and sun-
stroke. And so, under shadowing pepul and
baubul trees, among the boughs of which generations of the monkey people sit gravely contempla-
tive, we make our way home by the *ghaum* or
native town. Exquisitely knit, bottle-shaped nests,
that weaver-birds of last year have left, hang from
the pendulous branches of the acacias, and the
little pert black and yellow chitmucks or palm
squirrels are everywhere in evidence. Bulbuls are
already beginning to warble their spring love-song,
and a lark—rare and sweet—is finishing his morning lay before the sun gets too fierce even for him.
Herds of buffaloes, showing only the tips of their
long vulgar noses above the water's surface, are
soaking themselves in the blue lake, where, after
the manner of their kind, they would remain for
hours; and cream-coloured, high-humped kine, with
tall, backwards-sloping horns, are being watered at
its brink.

As we pass through the gate of the old fort the
aspect changes suddenly and completely. A vista

opens of long, tortuous, narrow streets of squalid
houses and dirty bazaars, from whence comes,
though it will be well to banish the fact from your
mind, your daily food.   White turbaned men and
queenly-looking *sari'd* women are buying and
selling or returning from the Temple, where they
have been making their morning *namuska*, or
offering of prayers with food and flowers.   Over
many of their doors are strings of the sacred
heart-shaped pepul leaves or a sprig of *tulsi*, the
symbol of the goddess Parvati.   Their household
shrines are visible within the open-fronted rooms,
whilst on one or two of the houses is imprinted an
open red hand, denoting that some ancestress had
brought honour upon her race by performing *sati*,
that some widow of a past generation had
voluntarily died by the flames of the same pile of
fire that had consumed her husband's body in
order to make reparation for his sins, and at the
same time crown her own life with an act of
superhuman self-sacrifice.   The touch of the *sati's*
hand, as she went to her death, was held to hallow
and bless all those on whom it was laid.

The old order changeth not in India, and Hindus
still lament over the law which banned the heroic
act enabling a wife—according to their belief—to
help not only her husband's soul, but to obtain
blessedness for her own; such a hard thing for a

woman to do in a land where the only apology for her existence is her probable marriage and possible maternity. Above all is it hard for the child-widows,—that product so uniquely Indian,— who are widows before they are wives. What a fate lies before them! Death (under the old law), drudgery, or a degradation and bondage worse than either.

Nevertheless, the mothers of sons in India receive their mead of affection and reverence. "We regard our parents," wrote Keshub Chunder Sen to Max Müller, "and especially the mother, as *sâkshât pratyakshadevata* (a present visible deity). Alive or dead we honour and revere her spirit." And Madam Saheb would tell you that she had known Indian widows who received nothing but honourable consideration at the hands of her husband's kinsfolk. But that, she will admit, was a concession, not a law-compelling requirement. And as we turned our backs on the *ghaum* and its strange, mysterious, hidden life, a shadow seemed to have fallen over the brilliancy of the Indian morning. Sorrow and pity possessed our souls—pity for the hapless little beings whose existences are stultified and sterilised by the stern and terrible exigencies of their own social laws.

IV.

AMONG THE DRAVIDIAN TEMPLES.

SECOND only to Benares in sanctity ranks the Temple of Seringham, the largest in India, and in comparison with which the temples of Japan—beautiful as they are in their own small decorative way—are as mere children's toys. By a bridge of thirty arches you reach, from Trichinopoli, an island which is formed by the bifurcation of the river Cauvery. Upon this island, which is seventeen miles in length and averages one and a quarter in width, there is room, not only for the town of Seringham, with its 30,000 inhabitants, but for a forest of banian and palm-trees, which engirdles and enshrines in its midst the Temple of Sri Rangam. Built in the early part of the eighteenth century and dedicated to Vishnu the Preserver, it is a notable example of the more modern Dravidian religious art of Southern India. So vast is it—for the Temple enclosure covers an area of more than one hundred and sixty acres—that its immensity is bewildering and its plan hard to grasp.

Across the top of a busy street, and occupying its entire width, there stretches the first great gateway by which you enter the rectangular enclosure. This gate is nearly fifty feet in height, and the passage through it, with ornamented and pilastered walls, is one hundred feet long. It might more fitly be termed a court. Monoliths are used as columns, and the horizontal slabs of granite which form its flat roof are also gigantic, measuring thirty feet in length. At the extremity of this passage a massive wall encloses the second inner court, which is occupied by priests and servers of the Temple. This is entered by a *gopura*, one of the gate-pyramids which are among the distinctive features of southern temples. Built here of the finest brick and covered with *shunam*,[1] they are mighty structures of piled-up tiers, each one of which is smaller than that below it. Each stage is a mass of sculptures in high relief—of gods and goddesses, snakes and devils, incarnations and symbolic animals, in a strange, grotesque confusion, barbaric but grand. Of these *gopuras* there are seventeen distributed about the walled enclosures of Seringham, graduating in size from those in the outermost and highest walls—in the north side of which there is one 152 ft. high, 130 ft. wide, and 100 ft. deep—to those which enclose the

[1] Hard and durable cement, like cream-coloured marble.

small cell containing the shrine, where they are comparatively insignificant.

There are seven degrees or "circles" of holiness between the outer bazaar and the innermost *adytum*. From court to court, each one walled, quadrangular and within the other, you pass from one gradation of sanctity to another till you reach the *Choultrie*, or "Hall of a Thousand Pillars." Of these granite pillars more than nine hundred and ninety, carved and bracketed, still remain, and in their midst is the Vimana or actual temple, a square, walled-up enclosure containing the shrine, the *garba griha*, or "Womb of the House," the first and final cause of this exuberance of art where the god is enthroned, and where none but Hindus may enter. All is gloom and shadow there, but from the porch which covers the entrance you may peer in, and in the remote darkness some dim and lurid lights will indicate the presence of the temple deity.

The temple elephants go trumpeting about the enclosures with strange devices like caste marks painted on their massive foreheads; and sacred cows, looking pensive and forlorn, and as though the burthen of their sanctity sat heavily upon them, stretch themselves wearily across the pavements, dreaming sweet dreams, doubtless, of the happy freedom and pleasant pastures which a less exalted station might have brought them. The *mela*, or annual festival, was in full swing, and the road through the palm grove, as well as the enclosure itself, was alive with pilgrims of all classes. We should have seen little of the Temple but for the Chief of the Police, who, with his superintendent, a stately Brahman, and a small body-guard of constables, made our course a clear one. The temple jewels, the famous pendants of diamonds and emeralds and diamond-studded coverings for the hands and feet of the idols, were already adorning the goddess in anticipation of to-morrow, the principal day of the festival, when a hundred and twenty thousand pilgrims will come to do *puja* at her shrine.

In the outside world of Seringham a pretty observance was being gone through this afternoon. Round the corner of a street a procession slowly wound its way. It was headed by some of the sacred elephants, followed by a band of native music, tom-toms and sitars. Then came some twenty or thirty white-robed Brahmans, and lastly a number of beautiful Brahman girls walking in double file. Brahman women of the south may be known by the way in which they wear their *saris*, one end of which they bring between the knees, thus producing the effect of a "divided skirt." It is by no means so graceful as the method adopted by the less exalted of their race, but it has the compensating recommendation of being *high caste.* Those Seringham maidens of high degree wore bunches of yellow flowers which peeped from under the heavy, braided bands of their lustrous black hair, and their supple forms and delicately moulded limbs seemed weighed down with collars, cinctures, bangles and anklets of finely wrought gold and silver. They wore ear-rings and jewelled studs in the sides of their nostrils. No women in the world, not even the most opulent of British matrons nor the most sumptuous of American millionaires, wear so many ornaments as do the women of Southern India. And none wear them with such grace and dignity, barbarous though the fashion be.

The elephants stopped and wheeled round to face the door of a modest-looking house, which nevertheless was the dwelling of a distinguished Brahman. When he came to the door they dropped on their knees in ponderous reverence, and then the Brahmans came forward and went through a courtly form of obeisance, which presumably took the place of an English hand-shake. Presently the daughters of the house came forth in homely, everyday raiment, and between them and their girl visitors there ensued an interchange of many pretty courtesies, the giving and taking of *pán,* or betel nut, the sprinkling with attar from long-necked, silver *surahis,* and the wreathing with garlands of champak blossom. It was all very like a scene from one of Imry Kiralfy's *spectacles;* and one was not a little surprised to learn that the occasion of so much ceremonial was nothing of greater moment than the delivery of an invitation to an impending wedding.

A mile and a half from Vishnu's Temple there is another and a smaller one dedicated to Jambukeshwar, or Shiva, the Jupiter among Hindu gods. It is on similar lines to those of the other, but of higher artistic merit. The *gopuras* are of granite, instead of brick and *shunam,* and an extra century of age has mellowed its tone. The bracketed columns and cornices of the inner courts are covered with rich symbolic carving, and about the whole place there is a delicious appearance of "uncare," greatly in contrast to the tawdry draperies and paintings which disfigured the great temple in honour of the festival.

The Brahmans and other worshippers, who moved about the enclosure in their own impassive and incurious fashion, the temple elephant, with his bells and his caste-marks over his small shrewd eyes, the palm-trees, like solemn, silent sentinels guarding the sacred place, and the *vahanas,* or triumphal cars—monster vehicles of carved wood used for carrying the gods and goddesses in procession—under their tiled sheds, coils of rope thick as a man's arm lying alongside wherewith to harness to them the hundreds of human beings who glory in the privilege of dragging the idols at festival time, — all lent themselves to the weird and fantastic spirit of the place.

The fervid, red light of the setting sun showed level through the palm-trees as we journeyed back to Trichinopoli, its glow and its heat falling still on the continuous stream of pilgrims who thronged along the road in thousands, on foot, in bullock-carts, and in *tongas.* There were weary women carrying heavy children on their hips and brass *lotas* under their arms; and men wrapped in *chuddahs* of the distinctive salmon colour which marks the pilgrim. There were fakirs with matted hair and little of covering except the *koupin* and the sacred Brahmanic cord across the left shoulder; and majestic men with staff in hand, the nobility of whose features, with hair uplifted from their brows and flowing over their shoulders, were reminiscent of ancient pictures of the Baptist. There were Tamuls of all degrees and types of beauty, well-poised heads, broad, open chests, and the stateliest and freest of gaits being the universal characteristic of this splendid Dravidian race.

The disfiguring caste-marks had assumed very exaggerated proportions in honour of the festival, and the married women, here as elsewhere in these districts, had "made themselves beautiful" by an application of turmeric or saffron on their (in many cases) comely, copper-coloured faces. Their ideal is apparently yellow on brown; ours is white on pink, or pink on white. After all, these things are matters of taste and custom. Doubtless from a colouresque point of view the Tamuls are right.

. . . . . .

Madura Temple is among the many things which make it worth while to come "o'er lands and seas" to visit India. Almost, as it were, beyond the grasp of a limited intelligence, the stupendous conception and barbaric glory of it is absolutely overwhelming and like some infinite thing. The Temples of Egypt pale before it, and Christian zeal has produced nothing to compare with it in magnitude. Except from an impressionist point of view none but an expert should attempt to describe it. The first sight of one of its colossal *gopuras*, rising to a height of one hundred and fifty feet or more in eleven graduated tiers, from a base on which sculptured elephants and horses stand out in stone, makes one feel breathless. Nothing in all the gigantic work is scamped or shirked. From base to ridge each range is a wealth of carving, and the topmost tier is as rich and as conscientiously wrought as any below it. Of such *gopuras* there are nine around the temple.

Another marvel, more like a fantastic dream than a reality, is the Pillared Hall, where you look through vistas which seem to vanish into remote distance, of countless bracketed, granite columns, all of which are monoliths and carved into every variety and elaboration of form and fancy. Some are covered with delicate Hindu ornament in low relief. A multitude of others—and there are nine hundred and eighty-five in all—have been sculptured into divinities and other mythical beings, and the effect is as though, by some magic power, the entire Hindu pantheon had been transformed into stone. Frightful and bizarre though most of them be, one cannot but reverence the enormous power and patient spirit of the work; and if there be truth in the theory that the vitality of an art school may be fairly gauged by its power in grotesquery, then indeed those Hindu master-sculptors were possessed by a spirit which did live and does live—whether for good or evil is beside the question. Fifteen of these columns have been walled up to form an enclosure for the shrine of Minakshi, the fish-eyed incarnation of Shiva's spouse, and out of the dimly-lighted distance,

٦ where she sits in unholy gloom, there came sounds
of murmuring voices which had more the semblance of incantations than of prayer.

Trimula, the most renowned among the rulers
of the Nayak dynasty, was a royal and religious
enthusiast to whom Southern India owes some
of her finest shrines. All Madura knows that
Shiva paid him annually, during his reign of thirty-
six years, a visit of ten days; and in gratitude for
this distinguishing mark of the god's favour he
built the Puda Mandapam, a mighty court of grey
granite, to serve as an ante-chamber or porch to
the Temple of Minakshi, his spouse. The hundred
and twenty-eight columns which support its massive roof are ranged in rows of four, and, again,
are fashioned into every conceivable form, human
and divine, animal and diabolic. Those which are
sculptured into rampant horses supporting richly-
carved brackets are unequalled anywhere for power
of conception and splendid grotesquery.

Why we were admitted within the great quadrangle which encloses the Teppa Kulam, or Tank
of the Golden Lilies, and not our bearer, whose
tarboosh proclaimed him a son of Islam, was at
first a mystery. We had crossed the sacred thres-
hold before remarking his absence. "Ah no," said
the young Hindu who had attached himself to us
at the gate of the Temple, "he Mohammedan and

cannot come in." And so the bitterness of old
resentment still lives, and retaliates thus, for the
sins of centuries, on the descendants of the hereditary enemies and religious persecutors against
whose fierce onslaughts and desecrations these
very *gopuras*, with their colossal, fort-like, flanking
walls may have, erstwhile, been built in defence
of the holy places. As for the Tank, the "golden
lilies" have ceased to be, if ever they existed,
except in the ready and poetic imagination of the
East. The roof of the broad arcade which runs
round the sacred lake is supported by stone *yali*,
or lions rampant. And there is a little chamber
within the walls which has a tragic story to tell
of the way in which the builder of it, Queen
Mangammol, was imprisoned by her subjects for
transgressing the Brahman law, and was done to
death by slow starvation. Tantalus himself was
not tortured with more refinement than was this
royal lady, whose tormentors intensified her death
agonies by daily placing within reach of sight and
smell all sorts of savoury viands. The Hindus of
later middle ages were by no means behind their
European contemporaries in the art of inventive
cruelty. It would hardly be just to say they
excelled them.

Under the arcade on one side of the Tank were
gathered a number of people, whose grouping and

colour made one yearn to be a painter of pictures. An arrogant-looking Brahman, naked to the waist, sat in oriental fashion against the wall preaching to a Tamul audience, who squatted around him in every degree of clothedness and unclothedness; the men loin-clothed and turbaned, or with their long hair knotted up behind, the fore-part of the head being shaved; the women in their *saris* of dark Indian red, apricot, or orange colour, worn with all the untrammelled dignity of their grace; and the children "mother-naked" and beautiful in form and colour.

Among the weight of ornaments worn by the women of Madura, their ear-rings are notable as being their sole disfigurement. They are the size of tulips, and the lobe of the ear is stretched to the length of two and a half inches. The process of stretching commences in infancy, and little children are to be seen with small wooden cubes, like bits of vine pencil, passed through the lobes of their ears. These cubes are gradually enlarged till the hole has become stretched to the dimensions demanded by the Maduran law of beauty.

Great pride do these Tamul women take in beautifying, as far as in them lies, not only the space of ground in front of their thresholds, but also the clay floors of their, often, hovel-like dwellings. First they wash them over with a

5

solution of the sacred cow-dung and liquid red clay; then they trace, with white powder, upon the red ground most beautiful and intricate designs. These patterns are all geometric, intersecting lines and circles, which no European draughts-man would think of drawing without the aid of instruments; and yet the Maduran women, by some inherited instinct, are able speedily to cover a space of many square feet by merely dropping the powder from between finger and thumb in the lines of the pattern which they wish to trace. The finishing touches of such as have florid tend-encies and *annas* to spare take the form of little "tees" (in golfing phrase) of clay at certain of the intersecting lines, wherein are stuck the heads of lily or marigold of the sacred yellow. Much may be gathered concerning the taste and capabilities of a Tamul housewife by the index of her thres-hold; for, as a rule, when the outside of the cup and platter were clean, the interior was in nowise disappointing. In Brahman houses, though the designs cover the entire floor, they are especially elaborated and beautified in front of where the Brahman master habitually sits.

The beauty of the country between Madura and Trichinopoli, and the voluptuous, unrestrained exuberance of its vegetation, recalled to one's mind the splendours of Cleopatra-like Ceylon. In addition to the ubiquitous bamboos and cactuses, the divi-divi, or umbrella tree, spread its flat branches like another cedar of Lebanon, and the banyans covered with their pendulous roots larger areas than one likes to write. There were hedges, too, of the curious milk-bush, the stalk-like foliage of which yields a milky substance, sweet and very poisonous, and said to have been used by Rajputs in days, happily, of long ago, when undesired daughters were born to them for whom they knew they should be unable to find husbands among their own blue-blooded race. Then, in order to obviate the disgrace of having to father, in the future, an unmarriageable daughter, a little juice of the milk-bush was cunningly smeared on the nurse's breast and the girl-baby sent to a friendlier home. Its cruel associations struck a note of discord in the midst of all that rich unfettered beauty of tropical nature, a beauty to which even the rice paddies contributed as they spread themselves over great tracts of the valleys near Madura into a sea of vivid green and stretched away into what seemed immeasurable distance, like the vast corn prairies of the "far west." And almost one could have thought that, like them, those sheets of verdant, waving crops, under such a sun and sky, might fertilise without much heed being paid to them. But the tillers of the soil would tell another tale, a tale of patient toil and laborious irrigation most primitive in its method. We sped by scores of them whilst they busily fed the thirsty land from the nearest tank or river. A long plank was fixed in the fork of a tree, at one end of which was slung a bucket; notches were cut in the plank to afford a foothold to the coolie who ran up and down it to counterpoise the bucket, which was thus lowered, filled, raised, and then emptied by a second coolie into a channel on the higher level.

As the valley contracts the hills gather themselves up at either side into great ramparts of protection to this fruitful plain. On our left the fortress-rock of Dindigal, with its tobacco factories and cheroot notoriety, looked down from its perch above us. Then through the rocky pass we laboured with much panting on the part of the engine, and soon, once again, we were within hail of another and a nobler rock-mount, that of "Trichi," which rears itself from the midst of the town, and from the temple-crowned summit of which there is to be seen a vision of such wide expanse and ardent beautifulness as can hardly be surpassed elsewhere in the plains of India.

V.

DRAVIDIAN TEMPLES.

IT is impossible to disintegrate the religious from the social and domestic life of India. Each is a component part of the others. The very ablutions of Hindus, the nature of the food they eat and the method of eating it, the systems upon which are based their domestic relations, their social observances, and the details of their daily work are all, more or less, matters of religious obligation. The whole conduct of their lives, from hour to hour, is shaped by two inexorable laws—the Brahmanic and the caste. And to meet the exigencies of their rites—rites which have endured for cycles of centuries, for Brahmanism is subject neither to vicissitudes nor development, unless Buddhism can be viewed as such, and no good Hindu would admit that conclusion—their temples must to a great extent be *planned* on similar lines.

But except in this respect the temples of Southern Dravidian India bear no semblance to the pagodas of Bengal, nor yet to those of the West, where the Chalukyan dynasty has left marvels of architectural beauty in the temples of its period, and where a fugitive Persian and an enduring Mohammedan influence have helped to temper and chasten the native religious art to a tone of greater moderation and refinement. Nowhere, however, is it conceived on anything like the same mammoth scale of grandeur, nor are the great *gopuras*, lake-like tanks, and vast pillared halls to be found north of Trichinopoli.

The temples of the south differ from each other rather in degree than in kind. There is a similarity, not to say monotony, in the tone and feeling of their work, extending from the earliest to the latest of them, which would be surprising were it not so entirely characteristic of the temper of the people. The Temple of Tanjore, because of its slight departure from this rule, and also because of its comparative antiquity—much of its work being laid at the door of the tenth century—is the most interesting of the group. Not that a few centuries more or less are of much account in this land of immutable ways. But the grey granite of Tanjore has divested itself of the gaudy tints which it, doubtless, like the others, wore in its youth, and has put on the mellow tone which belongs to venerable things and which is not to be found in all the redundant splendour of Madura and Seringham. Well-nigh a classic element may be found in the simpler ornament of its earlier work; whilst, on the other hand, the Subramanyi Shrine, dedicated to a son of Shiva, and dating only from the sixteenth century, has lost its outline in the exuberance of its florid decoration. It occupies a corner of the temple enclosure and corresponds in motive with the chapels of our old cathedrals. Fergusson pronounces it to be one of the most exquisite pieces of decorative architecture in Southern India. And he ought to know. But it is too suggestive of bridescake ornamentation to find favour with one who is not sufficiently initiated to discern and understand its architectural merits.

The noblest feature in Tanjore Temple, and one which makes it pre-eminent among the temples of the south, is the stupendous pagoda which rears itself, fashioned in fourteen richly sculptured, graduating stages, to a height of two hundred feet over the shrine of Shiva. This is one of the rare examples among the Dravidian temples of the central shrine occupying architectural prominence instead of being the meanest part of the buildings; and this arrangement goes far to constitute Tanjore, as a composition, completer and more harmonious than many of the greater temples.

Not far from this superb *vimana* is the shrine of
the Chandikasan, whose office it is to announce to
the temple deity the arrival of worshippers. The
gate-towers bear upon them the stamp of antiquity
in their comparative lack of height, though they
alone would be worth a pilgrimage, and, by those
who had not seen the colossal *gopuras* of the more
modern temples, would be regarded as gigantic.

One is told of the dynasties under which these
wonders of their own and all succeeding ages were
produced, but the generations have failed to hand
down any record of the men who built them, or
of the mighty intellects that conceived them,
almost reaching, it would seem, the summit of
human power. The kings of Tanjore and Vijay-
anager, we are told, gave their gold in a royally
lavish manner, but no word is written of the men
whose great brains contrived these colossal buildings, whose imaginations adorned them, whose
skilled hands fashioned them, and whose very
souls and personalities were wrought into them.
Through their work, truly, more may be learnt of
them than by aught that their mere names could
convey. And marvellous though these great monuments be, with what a sense of thankfulness and
refreshedness does one turn in memory to the
continent spirit and elevated thought which breathe
through the pure and noble outlines, the reserved

beauty and pregnant simplicity of an ancient Gothic church. Surely by their art you shall know them as well as by their works, and Hindu art, stupendous and splendid though it be, with its licence, its nautch-girls, its devilry, and its grotesquery, breathes not the spirit of light and purity as we know it.

Thus we sat moralising at the feet of Shiva's Bull, a monster "Nandi" sculptured from a block of black granite thirteen feet high, which sits like a huge watch-dog facing the temple of its master, when a wild-looking being approached and, through the medium of our guide, gave us to understand that the gods were about to be carried in procession from shrine to shrine, and that no unbelievers could therefore remain within the enclosure. Thus promptly and ignominiously driven forth, we betook ourselves to the great Shivaganga Tank, and there sat and watched the women who came in hundreds down the stone steps to fetch their water-supply for the night. To their knees in water they descended, and filling the brass *lotas*, most of which held three gallons, with the well-nigh opaque fluid which, in colour and consistency, was reminiscent of school-treat tea, they hoisted them on to their left hips, and after a little friendly feminine converse went off to their homes in twos and threes. Most of them took a draught of the holy and

uninviting beverage, which they quaffed gratefully
from the palms of their hands; and on our expressing a certain sorrow that they should absorb into
themselves anything so unclean, our Hindu guide
placidly remarked that, "This water bery sweet.
People like it bery much." So true is it that
"beauty is in the eye of the gazer."

One girl, more graceful than the rest, we found
especially alluring as she stood ankle-deep in the
water on the tank steps and went through many
pretty *puja* observances. First she sipped a little
from the hollowed palms of her beautiful brown
hands; then a few drops were sprinkled over her
bowed head. Each elbow was then touched with
the sacred water, and so was each limb and each
joint during the course of her purifications. Her
every action was full of delicate, flexuous grace,
and so superbly was she moulded that she might
have been some exquisite, animated statue—a
second Galatea—and no less pictorial for being in
copper-bronze instead of in white marble.

Tanjore city is essentially "native." There is
no European element to destroy its oriental character. From the quaint "bits" of Hindu architecture which arrest you at every few yards in
passing along the streets, to the artists who squat
on their verandahs and solemnly beat out wondrous
repoussé patterns on silver and copper vessels, and

to the little brown boy of three who stood also on *his* verandah, full of rice, and fresh from the much-approved oil-tub which had left him dripping from the crown of his head to the soles of his feet and shining like polished oak, there was no discordant note.

From the door of a small house a procession was starting of gaily-clothed men followed by a number of bullock-carts laden with provisions of all sorts—fruit, pán-leaves, betel, and sweetmeats. The two last carts were laden each with a monster metal pan, like boilers, filled with rice. There was music too, if a confusion of sound proceeding from horns and tom-toms, each of which knew but one note, could be so described. With these accompaniments they were "carrying rice" from the home of her future husband to a little girl-bride whose wedding ceremonies, lasting over many days, were duly dragging along their tedious course. Stern reality was henceforth to replace the nursery drama of her childhood. For we are told by those who know that though their dolls are their chief pastime, many of the favourite games of Indian girls are based upon this, to them, all-absorbing subject of matrimony. Sometimes, for example, one of the company assumes the part of a would-be mother-in-law and comes, with all her female relatives, to the house of the little maid

whom she desires to secure as a bride for her son.
Into her ear she pours a tale of this imaginary
son's countless perfections of mind and body, the
interview generally ending in the honour of the
alliance being declined—a proud moment for the
maiden, who in after-life, when the play has become a reality, shall have no voice in the matter.

Again, a precocious young person of eight or
nine will assume the airs of a bride-elect, and the
game will consist in recounting to her playmate
"mother" all the *articles de luxe* which she desires
for her *trousseau*—shawls, *saris*, broideries, bangles,
cinctures, anklets, necklaces, and ear-rings, not to
mention "toilet requisites," *henna* for her nails, and
soorma for her eyes, saffron for her complexion,
and sandal-wood paste, oil of sesame, attar and
kusa wherewith to anoint and perfume her small
person.   And so these joyless-looking little beings
recreate themselves—hardly, to English notions,
after a manner healthy or invigorating, but one
which is necessarily the outcome of their forced,
exotic rearing, and of the continuous instilling into
their empty little minds, by way of education, that
marriage is the aim and end of their existence, and
maternity their *raison d'être*.

    .   .   .   .   .

A contented mind is at all times, we are told,
a great gain, but to those whose lines fall among

dâk bungalows such a possession is a very mine of
wealth. To be able, after a long and fatiguing
journey, to find rest and refreshment in an upright,
wooden-seated chair and to regard with gratifica-
tion a somewhat rickety and aggressively hard
charpoy, or bedstead, whereupon to unfurl your
mattress and repose your weariness, argues a
robust moral tone for the attainment of which
one is tempted to feel, with a smack of self-com-
placency, that it is almost worth while to come
from West to East. Frequently, however, this
Spartan spirit is rudely checked by the appearance
of a repast out of all harmony with the stern
simplicity of the surroundings, which the *khansaman* will serve with as much state as a ragged,
coarse table-cloth and broken-down appliances will
admit of. The singular aptitude with which Indian
servants respond to the large requirements of the
saheb loque speaks eloquently of their adaptive
capacity and ready apprehension. The same man
who lives day by day, year in year out, on rice,
beans, and *ghee*—that terrible *ghee!*—with a sleek,
well-nourished result, not only takes it as a matter
of course that the *saheb* cannot dine, under any
circumstances, on *less* than five courses, but is
nearly always equal to the occasion. His mutton
is not four-year-old Southdown, and the inevitable
moorghee is often put to death whilst the spit is

waiting for it, but the regulation number of *plats*
is always forthcoming, and the more exacting the
saheb's requirements, the more honourable does he
appear in the eyes of his menials.

But a worse thing than a *dâk* bungalow may
befall you, and that is *no dâk* bungalow. At
Chidambaram we had managed, by the aid of a
stool, borrowed from the station-master, to crawl
over the immovable back seat of a *jutka* which
had lost its only step. In this springless and
penitential vehicle, clutching spasmodically at the
side rails, we proceeded for three miles along a
glaring road, the white dust of which reflected the
torrid rays of the relentless afternoon sun, through
the town, past the great *gopura* of the temple, and
so on to the bungalow, only to find it already
occupied by the district collector and his sister,
who were then at the temple. This was crushing
news. But the man whom we took to be the
khansaman in charge, and who, we eventually
found to our consternation, was Mr. Cumming's
own servant, undertook to give us some dinner
"when the *saheb* and missee dined." I threw out
a mild suggestion that "the *saheb* and missee"
might very reasonably object to the privacy of
their room and table being invaded by absolute
strangers. But this idea was indignantly rejected.
"Must make friendly," said the man; "all one

caste, must help each other." This, doubtless, was strictly in accordance with Hindu ethics, but I could not feel the confidence that I should have wished in its universal acceptance and practice among Christians. Eventually I had reason to be sorely ashamed of my lack of faith in the charity of my kind; for on the return of Mr. Cumming and his sister they not only took us in, sheltered and fed us, but through his agency we witnessed what few except Hindus ever see—viz., the carrying in procession within the temple enclosure, which covers thirty-two acres, of the gods and goddesses on their great annual festival day.

Mr. Cumming's presence at such a time was official, and we were tolerated under the shadow of his wing. Many thousands of pilgrims thronged the enclosure, and many more thousands had been scared from coming by the dread rumour that cholera lurked in the district. As it was, the people swarmed on every coign of vantage—on to the bases of the four great gate-towers, on to the roof of Vermas' exquisite miniature shrine,—car-like with its sculptured wheels and horses and its graceful dancing figures,—amid the "thousand pillars" which form the great hall, and up the steps leading to the Temple of Ganesh, the elephant-headed son of Shiva. They clung to Subramanya's stone elephants and sat on his peacocks. The porches, the walls, the roofs, wherever there was an elevation and a foothold, there they were congregated in a glorious confusion of vivid colour. It was a grim and humiliating spectacle when the frightful images were brought forth from their darkened shrines, and, decked in jewels, sapphires, and diamonds of enormous size and priceless worth, were carried under canopies on great triumphal cars whilst fuming censers were tossed in front of them. The temple band of horns and tom-toms made cruel discord, and banners and peacock plumes were waved on this side and that, whilst nautch-girls, "in spangled skirts and bells," danced before the gods in the advancing procession.

In Chidambaram the god is honoured in his incarnation of Natasan, or "god of dancing," and is represented as a naked giant with the four arms distinctive of Shiva, and one leg poised in the air. All good Hindus know that a great Rajah of the Chola dynasty in the tenth century saw Shiva dancing on the sands with Parbati, his spouse, and to commemorate the vision he built the golden shrine. Another grateful monarch, "the golden-coloured emperor," so named by reason of his leprosy, enlarged and beautified Shiva's Temple as an act of thanksgiving for the miraculous cure of his disease by bathing in the sacred tank.

For this purpose he made a pious pilgrimage to Chidambaram from the north, and brought in his train three thousand Brahmans. Quite that number might have made their *puja* without over-crowding in the vast walled-in lake.

And so the world has to thank those royal devotees not only for fine examples of gratitude—a rare virtue—but for superb specimens of Indian art. The four gate-pyramids are the oldest in Southern India and full of the beauty of their kind—mighty, forcible, weird, devilish, licentious, fabulous, grotesque it may be, but telling a tale of gigantic genius, of labour that knew no weariness, and of a faith which might remove mountains, a faith the iron-bound rule of which entirely precludes the flexible adaptivity which argues vitality, but which, nevertheless, possesses an endurance stern and adamantine, the endurance of granite or basalt, and, like them, though capable of great things, "has no true life in it."

VI.

AMONG THE SNOWS.

WITH a sigh of relief and a profound *Deo gratias*
we shook the dust of Calcutta from our feet.
Setting aside its bright social aspect and the
kindness of newly-made friends, there is little to
detain travellers there. In place of meagrely-
made, tawdrily-dressed Madrasees, we had tall
and dignified Bengalees, the "Scots of India," as
they have been called, by reason of their intellectual capacity, their literary activity, and their
comparative lack of artistic sense, who drape their
chuddahs about them like togas, and whose un-
covered heads, except for their thick black hair,
worn short after the English fashion, defy the
fierce tropical sun as daringly as did the twenty
Englishmen whom we saw in Madras playing a
cricket match at mid-day, whilst the thermometer
registered a hundred and thirty degrees. Government House is a more regal-looking dwelling than
Buckingham Palace, and the evening drive on the

Red Road, with its gorgeous natives and its smart
Europeans, its sumptuous carriages and, often,
Rosinanti-like horseflesh, is unique and entertaining.
So are the races. And the Botanical Gardens at
Garden Reach are perhaps the finest in the world.
But nothing can compensate for the evil odours
which permeate the city, more especially the
European and more fashionable quarters, and
which seem to enter into and nauseate one's inner
being. Cologne is a rose-garden compared to
Calcutta.

At the risk, therefore, of having to face the
chilling fogs which often hang over Darjeeling in
this month of February, we determined to air our
lungs amid the "hills," as the Anglo-Indians call
the loftiest mountains in the world. A dinner on
board a Ganges ferry-boat, a night's journey from
Sara Ghât—luxurious as only a night's journey on
board an Indian train can be—and on the following
morning you are turned out of your comfortable
berth at Siliguri, breakfasted, and packed into a
compartment (rather like a pen) of a small toy-like
train. How the miniature engine is to lift you
seven thousand and odd feet above your present
level seems a problem. But in blind faith you
pack yourself and your luggage, which in India,
because of the facilities offered, assumes proportions which would be tolerated by no other railway

companies in the world, into as small a compass as possible and commence the aerial journey.

So marked did we find the change in the racial characteristics of the people on leaving Siliguri that we might have crossed a frontier. The nobler and more refined Aryan type was left behind to give place to the broad faces, flattened noses, slit eyes, and yellow skins which mark the Mongolian origin of the aboriginal hill tribes of Sikkim. Only the Mechis can exist within the seven miles of verdant level tract which engirdles the base of the Himalayas. In the Terai—a Persian word meaning damp—wild birds of countless varieties have their home, and there is pasture abundant for the herds of the Mechi, who, stunted and sallow though they be, are so acclimatised to the malaria that the majority die of those who migrate to the hills for the purpose of labouring in the tea plantations.

We crossed this verdant and miasmal plain, and having reached the base of the mountains, our plucky little engine began to wind its sinuous way up the two-foot gauge, gliding smoothly round inner curves and hugging great headlands; now following a zigzag track,—like a ribbon folded back on itself,—where the turns are so acute that the train has to be backed to the higher level, and again creeping along a narrow gorge with sheer heights

on one side and profound depths on the other;
but ever and always persistently, steadily mount-
ing, never exceeding seven miles an hour—*ohne
Hast ŭnd ohne Rast*—up and around the forest-
clad mountains, with never the aggravation of a
tunnel to obstruct the fair vision of the distant, sea-
like plains and the towering peaks overhead.

Straight through the villages of the hill country
the railway cuts its route, the train stopping
frequently in the centre of the bazaars, where the
inhabitants, principally Lepchas, with pigtails and
pleasant though grotesquely ugly faces, are busily
bargaining and trading with each other or with the
Nepaulese Tibetans, who bring rock-salt, musk,
ponies, etc., to barter for pieces of cloth and
tobacco. Both form and face bear witness to the
fact that one and all spring from the same race,
and only by their dress are they to be differentiated.
The Lepchas, by way of religion, practise a debased
form of Buddhism, and round about the huts of the
more pious among them are erected tall bamboo
poles with rag streamers floating from them, a
most efficacious method of propitiating evil spirits.

Each hour of the journey lifted us a thousand
feet higher and brought with it a change in the
flora and fauna of the mountains. Gradually the
tropical and savagely luxuriant vegetation of their
lower belt gave place to a plant life equally abun-

dant, but one indigenous to temperate regions.
Many of the sombre mountain giants of the lower
zone are festooned and clad, to their own ultimate
destruction, with superb parasitic climbers—vines,
bignonias, convolulus, and the gorgeous pothos—
more beautiful often than the doomed trees which
they wrap in their deadly embrace. Others are,
as it were, knit together by interlacing creepers
which hang cable-wise from branch to branch,
whilst their trunks are made to nourish great
bunches of orchids, lycopodia, and pendulous
mosses which have rooted themselves in the
niches of their bark. Everywhere there are
acacias, cassias, plantains, and fig-trees of many
varieties. Screw-pines twist their straight stems
upwards to an immense height, waving their
crowns of leaves, sometimes ten feet long, on
this side and that. The stately *lumba putte*,
or "long leaf," put forth their clusters of dark
red blossom at the terminal of each gigantic
branch. Clumps of purple-stemmed bamboos
crown the hills, and prosaic, stiff-looking tea
plantations cover many slopes and fill many
valleys.

At the height of four thousand feet, a compact,
opaque, grey cloud was waiting to receive us, and
not only did it envelop us in a damp and chilling
embrace, but it very effectually veiled everything

beyond a radius of eight or ten yards, in spite of
which we recognised within range of sight some
home friends—oaks, chestnuts, walnuts, and laurels.
But such, by that time, was our condition of
cramped and chilled physical misery that all
spirit of enthusiasm had evaporated, and even
the lordly cedars, the *cryptomeria japonica*, that
came towering and crowding around us out of
the white cloud fog, hardly aroused in us any
ardour of admiration.

On steaming fussily into Darjeeling station
nothing was to be seen but coolies, principally
women, who are practically the beasts of burthen
in this district. To my horror I saw my large
cabin trunk, weighing some six or eight stones,
being slung on to the back of a little Bhutea
woman about four feet high. A strap attached
to the trunk was passed across her forehead, and
under this incubus she started, with a waddling
gait, through the fog up the mountain pathway
leading to the hotel. I had to halt many times
for breathing space on the way, whilst she trudged
steadily on without gasp or sigh. It was her
daily portion, and one has to become accustomed,
in and about Darjeeling, to the barbarous sight of
these small women and still smaller children performing the tasks of labourers and navvies, carrying
on their backs loads of stone and baulks of timber

up and down hill always, for here there is no such
thing as level ground.

For many days we waited, knowing well that if
the clouds which lay piled and morose below us
and round about us would permit, we might look
down into profound valleys and over the clustering
heads of lower mountains. We knew also, that
far above the grey veil which encompassed us
there dwelt a mighty Presence, for a vision of
which we thirsted. We looked, and longed, and
shivered in the bosom of the unfriendly fog until
one blessed morning, when we rose as usual with
the dawn, we could hardly believe our eyes on
seeing the manifestation which met them. Sunlit
clouds, lying level and looking like an ocean of
ochreous vapour, still filled the valleys and en-
veloped the lower mountains, the heads of which
rose from their midst like islands. But far above
and beyond them towered a vision of reachless,
death-white realms — the Himalayan range of
snow-clad giants. They seemed like stupendous
ramparts, those piled-up snowy domes and peaks,
separating this from another world. And yet so
little of earth had they about them, so majestic
were they in their loneliness, so awe-compelling in
their cold, calm purity, that one well-nigh felt in
the presence of the Eternal.

There, then, were the sanctuaries of the everlasting snows, immutable during centuries of years and cycles of centuries, looking down on the common things of earth from their solemn heights, unveiling their mystery at rare and holy seasons— these, the most sublime of God's creations short of the angelic choirs and the soul of man. What are temples made with hands, even the most wonderful in this wonderful land, in comparison with these! And yet surely the architects of India must have shaped their conceptions on the same lines that nature has cast for them in their own favoured country, lines of such vast magnitude as are not to be found elsewhere in the world.

For many succeeding days the Himalayan cloud-spirits were propitious, and for an hour after each solemn dawn lifted their diaphanous silvery curtains to disclose the glories beyond the veil. On one such morning Miss N—— and I determined to ride to the top of Tiger Hill, six miles distant and a thousand feet higher, in the hope of seeing the crown of Everest, the patriarch and monarch of all the mountains of the earth, eight hundred feet higher than Kinchingunga, and more than a hundred miles distant. We rode fast, for we knew it was a race with the clouds, and outstripped our *syces*, swift of foot though they were, by two miles. We were just in time to see the last gleam of the imperial head as it merged into great volumes of opaque white cloud which had been indolently creeping over the intervening kingdom of snows. A strange contrast that kingdom showed, in its deathlike beauty, to the vital loveliness of the leagues of sun-bright valley and hill country which separated us from it. And even as we looked, the clouds amassed themselves below us, filling the valleys and girdling the bases of the entire range, causing them to seem suspended between a cloud-ocean which submerged and blotted out the world below and the inimitably blue sky above.

As we stood, without speech, drinking in the beautifulness of this wonderland, we were startled by a sound which came, in the silence of the mountains, apparently from the jungle only a few yards from us. "Did you hear that?" said my friend. "Yes," said I, rather faintly. "Did you ever hear anything like it except in a menagerie?" "No," I answered, in a quailing voice; "shall we go down?" "Well," said Miss N——, who is cast in sterner mould than I, "it is very disappointing to have to leave the mountains, but even *they* would not compensate for an unforeseen encounter with a tiger.' Another growl decided us. With blanched faces we promptly made for the bridle-path which led down through the jungle, and as its narrowness and steepness compelled us to ride in single file and at foot pace, there ensued a polite contention as to who should go *last* and risk being pounced upon by the bloodthirsty beast in our rear, each feeling constrained to an act of self-immolation in favour of the other. And so we sped down at the risk of our necks, gaining reassurance only on meeting the *syces* a mile lower down.

In cool blood, and on ascertaining that no tiger had so much as been heard of on Tiger Hill "within the memory of the oldest inhabitant," we came to the conclusion that we would observe strict reticence concerning this little incident. But, in a rash and misguided moment, I unburthened my soul of its secret to the *burra saheb*, who, after the fashion of men and husbands, has ceased not to jeer and cast that tiger in our teeth on every available occasion. Great, therefore, was our exultation, on learning a few days subsequently, that tracks of a bear had been found in that very jungle, and that a *shikar* had been organised for the purpose of slaying him.

And yet I am not sure that that fictitious tiger shocked one's nerves in a much less degree than did a genial American globe-trotter who, on another occasion, rode with us to the same vantage point. We had ridden out under the awaking sky of the early morning hours, and as the pale lustrous dawn graduated into perfect day, and the sun rose glorious from behind the snows like an "avenging fire-god," causing the death-white Himalayas to kindle and glow in the light of his presence, a vision which made one speechless and almost breathless, our Transatlantic cousin remarked in a tone of calm finality, "Wall, that's what *I* call vurry neat." To have such a remark hurled at you in an aggressively "Yankee" accent, when you are in a state of great mental exaltation and excitement, is like receiving a cold douche with your pulse beating at fever height. But a sense of the comic side of the situation— oh, good spirit of comedy, how would the world fare without you?—came to the rescue, causing an instant reaction, and one could not but look with a certain degree of awe on a being who could regard nature in her sublimest moods from such an impervious standpoint.

.   .   .   .   .   .

The incongruity and discordance here between inanimate nature in all its glorious magnificence, and the low ignoble type of the humanity whose abiding land it is, thrusts itself forcibly on the notice. Among no known races, probably, are there to be found peoples of a lower order of intelligence than are those of the Himalayan hill tribes. Of a strongly-defined Mongolian type, they are all more or less of Tibetan origin and ugliness. They all speak dialects of the Tibetan tongue, and their social framework, quasi-savages though they be, is based on Tibetan manners and customs. Except among the Lepchas, the primitive inhabitants of Sikkim, in whom the moral tone is many degrees higher than in most of the Himalayan tribes, polyandry is commonly practised, and modesty and cleanliness are words which convey no significance to them. Trading, tea, and labour make Darjeeling a central resort for them all—for, to give them their due, they are very industrious—and the weekly Sunday fair, when a crowded gathering of the clans takes place in the bazaar, is the opportunity for seeing them in all their wealth of ornaments and excessive dirt. The wiry, agile Nepaulese, who have colonised in Darjeeling to obtain employment in the tea plantations, form the largest proportion. They are skilful handicraftsmen, and their military reputation is splendidly upheld by their ruling clan, the Ghoorkhas. The murderous-looking *kukeri*, or curved knife, which they all carry, might well inspire dread, were it not for the amiable nature and gentle ways which belong to them.

There is also a large admixture of Bhuteas, the hewers of wood and drawers of water, unskilled,

and amongst the lowest of the tribal peoples.
Repute says they are much given to intoxication,
both men and women, and one is glad to know
that they do not owe this vice altogether to British
association and whisky, as they manufacture their
own "strong water" from rice and *murwah* or
millet. The poorest coolie among them all is laden
with silver ornaments set more or less richly with
turquoises, and sometimes beautifully designed and
wrought. Here, for instance, is a man thickly
coated with dirt, whose sole garment is a long
tunic, the fabric of which seems held together by
the accumulation of many ages' grease and filth.
In its upper folds, above the belt, are stowed away
an indiscriminate store of food—fruit, rotten fish,
and rice—together with many tempting *articles de
vertu*, which, on seeing a *memsaheb*, he promptly
produces from this unsavoury receptacle and
thrusts before her eyes. If these fail to tempt,
he tears from his neck a silver reliquary, a flat
box two or three inches square, encrusted with
turquoises, and containing a little idol or the relics
of a mahatma, and intimates that this also he is
willing to part with at a price. His prayer-wheel,
likewise, which he had been religiously twirling,
may be yours, or the knife from his belt, or the
enormous ear-rings, like old-fashioned bell-pulls,
from the distorted lobes of his wife's ears.

Here, again, is a Tibetan woman, her noseless
and slit-eyed offspring lashed, in a bamboo basket,
on to her back in approved Mongolian fashion, her
long and abundant black hair hanging in two
ample plaits behind, her face covered, mask-wise,
with a thick black pigment which has been
smeared on previous to crossing Jelep le Pass
to protect her skin from the keen frost, and
which it has apparently escaped her mind to
wash off. Whilst one of her husbands is bartering
a flock of sheep for cotton yarn and tobacco she
seizes the opportunity of greeting you with what
is doubtless meant for a pleasant smile, then she
scratches her ear or perhaps thrusts out her tongue.
These proceedings are calculated to startle the
uninitiated who are ignorant that they are merely
the Tibetan form of salutation, and that, far from
wishing to be rude, the sole desire of the grinning
lady is to ingratiate herself in the hope of dis-
posing of her heavy silver girdle to the best possible
financial advantage. Meanwhile, the husband, a
wild-looking, beardless being with streaming hair,
having completed his own bargain, joins us to
assist in our transaction, and with a view to
offering suggestions to your male friends for
future *bals costumés*, you make mental notes of
his "get up"—a blanket robe secured round his
waist by a leathern belt from which hangs the

entire paraphernalia of his domestic economy, pipes, tobacco pouch, some deadly-looking knives, a wooden drinking-cup, chopsticks, tinder-box, and tweezers, the latter for the purpose of removing every hair which threatens to mar the harmony and beauty of his unwashed countenance. Add to this, silver and turquoise rings on fingers and toes, silver amulets, and rows of coral beads, and you have the Tibetan trader in all the glory and wealth of his war-paint.

It is refreshing to turn from these fantastic, unsightly, dirty beings to a Lepcha woman, a tartar every inch of her, with yellow skin and pig-tailed hair, but pleasantly ugly like the Japanese, and comparatively cleanly, though evidence goes to prove that the people even of her tribe have an invincible repugnance to water, at least for ablutionary purposes. If you can but banish from your mind that her daily food is made up of such inconsiderate trifles as you would not allow your dogs to approach—snails, caterpillars, bracksie cattle, in fact anything that can be found, cleanly or foul—you would regard her as a pleasant and even picturesque object in her gaily-striped skirt, her cloak of divers hues, and her coronal of red cloth thickly sown with pearls and turquoises. You sordidly long to possess yourself of her girdle, which is formed of numberless silver chains, or of the amber beads or other neck ornaments with which she is laden; for to-day she is "clothed in the garments of her gladness," in honour of the weekly festival. You know that she has been purchased by her husband, either with rupees or with the sweat of his brow, but you also have the satisfaction of knowing that she has been properly and decorously married—that is to say, she has performed the solemn rite of holding in her hands a hen, whilst the bridegroom held a cock, that with one stroke of the knife the officiating priest decapitated both the unhappy birds, and augured from the direction in which their blood flowed as to the future felicity or infelicity of the newly-wedded pair. The former may fairly be assumed, not only because of the rigorous regard in which the Lepchas hold their marriage vows, but because of their good-natured and easy-going temperaments.

Lepcha wives are the stronger vessels, and undertake most of the heavy responsibilities of life both at home and abroad. Whilst they do coolie work, carrying on their backs baulks of timber and loads of stone that would stagger a British labourer, their worse halves may be seen tranquilly smoking their hookahs by the wayside, or gambling and chatting cheerfully with their neighbours. It is a sight to be deplored, and yet in

7

this case it seems to work for the common good.
And madam's biceps have by no means gathered
strength unto themselves to no purpose.   If all
tales be true, conjugal chastisement is frequently
administered in a wholesome, temperate, and
effectual manner, and received in a patient and
right spirit by the Lepcha lords of creation, who;
when they will, can work well and are conspicuous
for their weight-carrying powers and mountaineer-
ing endurance.

If the Lepchas were asked what religion they
professed they would tell you they were Buddhists,
but few would know even the meaning of the term.
Beyond their reverence for and faith in the supernatural power of their *lamas* to work them both
good and evil, their spirit of tolerance towards
those of other religions, and their absolute belief
in the transmigration of souls, there is little of
Gautama's teaching left to the merry, drunken,
honest, careless Lepchas.   But if he could see and
hear the things that are taught and done in his
name all the world over, surely even *his* Nirwana
would be disturbed.   The so-called religion of
these tribes is one wholly of fear—a propitiation
of evil powers, who they believe inhabit the
mountains, rivers, rocks, and trees.   And indeed,
from their point of view, it must be hard to say
which are the more terrifying, those demons which

they do *not* see, or the frightful, revolting images of "gods" which they do.

Not far from Lebong Spur, the camping-ground of the Tibetans, and some five miles from Darjeeling, there is a Buthean *lamasary* perched—where *lamas* love to be—on the side of a hill somewhat difficult of access; at least it would be so were it not for the dauntless little Tibetan ponies, to which neither the steepest of mountain bridle-paths nor the weightiest of riders seem to present any obstacle. A ride of about a mile from Lebong, through a copse of rhododendrons, magnolias, laurels, and camellias, brought us to a miserable *bustee,* or village of mud-huts, which clings, in all the integrity of its native, unspeakable filth, to the hillside. Over the roof of each dwelling, an eruption of bamboo poles, waved cotton prayer-rags. A small forest of these pious ensigns also sprang from a barn - like building which occupied a grove a little apart from the *bustee,* and which we knew was the *gompa* when we saw a *lama* squatting in the vestibule and mechanically turning one of the great prayer-wheels which were suspended there. This particular cylinder was six feet in height, and we begged the *lama,* with all deference, to continue his orisons. With each revolution of the wheel a bell rang, whilst he dreamily and drowsily intoned the refrain, *Om Mani Padma Hom*—" Hail to him of the Lotus and Jewel."

A few turns satisfied our curiosity, and, at the same time, added to the *lama's* merit, and then, with the geniality for which Buddhists generally are conspicuous, he proceeded to show us the treasures of his *gompa*. But to us his precious manuscripts were as sealed books, and his idols calculated to produce bad dreams. Very grue- some also were the kettledrums fashioned from human skulls, commonly supposed to be those of faithless husbands whose spirits shall know not re-birth until their desecrated craniums cease to be put to this base use. Trumpets likewise were shown to us made out of men's thigh-bones; though what crime had incurred this minor penalty tradition sayeth not. Musical instruments of similar fabric and with the same joyous and ex- hilarating associations are offered for sale in the bazaar, so it is to be feared that many headless spirits of unrest are at large in Sikkim, each one doubtless haunting the abiding-place of his own skull. In the *gompa* these human relics are kept on the altar, together with conch shells, peacocks' feathers, bells, brazen cups, and sprigs of juniper, the latter to be mixed with charcoal and used as incense.

The *lama* of the *gompa* spoke no language that

we could understand, but a day or two later we met, in the house of a German who is about to join the Buddhist priesthood, a red-capped *lama* who had just returned from Tibet. A young Bhutean *pundit* was also present who interpreted for us, and who, apparently, was better versed in the mystical teaching of Buddhism than was the *lama* himself. The latter was a stout, comfortable-looking gentleman in a red cloak and skull-cap, with twinkling, good-natured, and rather sly-looking eyes. The *pundit* was young, earnest, and full of the fire of zeal. He was full, also, of blind credulity in the supernatural power of *lamas* to work good and evil at their will, even to those at a remote distance. He eagerly told us of *Shooshoks* (re-incarnations) in Tibet who could knead a boulder stone as though it were dough, and who had but to will a man's death in order to accomplish it. He earnestly defended the doctrine of metempsychosis on the grounds of its reasonableness, urging that a merciful God could never expect a man to save his soul in the short course of one human lifetime.

Meanwhile the *lama's* little bead-like eyes twinkled amiably as he looked inquiringly from one of us to the other, and he complacently exhibited to us the small implement, like a miniature sceptre with a nine-sided crown at its top, through the instrumentality of which *lamas* are commonly believed by their flocks to be able to hypnotise whom they will. We asked with deference for the reason of the attitude of rigorous exclusiveness adopted by the Grand *Lama* of Lassa (the Tibetan Pope and King) towards foreigners, and met with the prompt answer, "Because first would come missionaries, then would come whisky, and lastly would come soldiers." Having cast this stone at us in a gentle and pacific fashion, they again retreated into the ambush of theological conference, or rather assertion, always based on inconsequential, discursive, and shallow arguments, expressed in fluent and excellent English, and with a childish simplicity, absolute personal self-reliance, and entire freedom from arrogance and bitterness. We parted excellent friends, but with surprise and regret on their part that they had been unable to persuade us to Buddhism.

VII.

TWO PHASES OF HINDUISM.

A VERY short sojourn among the natives of India suffices to convince one that the religious and social life of Hindus is one and indissoluble, so closely interwoven are their domestic with their religious laws and observances. But not perhaps till after a visit to ancient and classic Benares, the holiest of their holy cities, is it possible fully to realise the tenacity of hold which, in spite of the tendency of the more cultured among them to lapse into Atheism, Brahmanism still possesses on the masses among the peoples of India. There, are to be seen its weird and fantastic rites practised in all their fulness by throngs of people of every age and caste, the hurrying multitude of pilgrims daily coming and going to cast their sins into the broad swelling bosom of holy Mother Gunga, or to obtain, by immersion in her turbid waters, yellow with the accumulated mud of some thousands of miles' washings, some present earthly gift or relief

from suffering. *Ghât* after *ghât* (broad flights of
stone or marble steps), to the number of forty-
seven, line her incurving shore, and lead down to
the river from the city, which is piled up in irregular
buildings on the higher level. Many Rajahs have
built palaces on her banks for their souls' sakes,
and as each one has built irrespective of his
neighbour, besides having made additions at odd
times to his own domains, in a delightfully free
and inconsequent fashion, the result is a broken
and very pictorial line of buildings, some princely
and some in decay, for, after the manner of the
East, where they have fallen there they lie. The
wall of the Temple, for instance, which crowns
Sindia's *ghât*, is riven from top to base, and its
massive walls and cornices are many degrees out
of the perpendicular, whilst the domes and minarets
of Aurungzebe's mosque rise majestically behind
the ruins.

Each *ghât*, with its adjacent buildings, has its
own speciality. One possesses a well, the waters
of which are peculiarly efficacious in curing fever
and dysentery. At another, serpent-worship is
practised, the spreading boughs of a pepul-tree
shading the stone images of writhing, crawling
wickedness which the people delight to honour.
Sitla *ghât* rejoices in a goddess who averts small-
pox from her clients through the practical agency

of her human coadjutors of the gardener caste, the recognised professional inoculators in India, who receive all the offerings made to their patron goddess; and the presiding deity of Someshwar, a "lady doctor," makes the victims of elephantiasis— a common disease among the natives of India— her special care.

Shiva, the Jupiter of Hindu pantheism, is commonly believed to ride about the city on an invisible dog, and at his *ghát*, where he sits in state with his four outspread hands and his face of silver, the image of his canine steed is kept regularly supplied with votives in the form of small sugar dogs made for the purpose by the neighbouring confectioners. This *ghát* would find many votaries among the promoters of "Homes for Lost Dogs," for barley cakes are daily supplied by the holy *gosain*, whose office it is, to all the pariah dogs in need of a meal.

Presumably the European superstition concerning the evil omen attached to peacocks' feathers is reversed in this continent, as the Brahman in attendance at Sitla *ghát* very considerately waves over you a fan of the beautiful jewelled plumes in order to ward off evil spirits. If, at the same time, they could dispel the deadly fumes and nauseous odours that arise from the sacred and polluted river not far from this point, the result of an enormous drain emptying into it the accumulated filth of Benares, the well-disposed gods and goddesses might be enabled with greater facility to work the cures for which they are besought with such earnest faith.

To sail down the Ganges at the setting of the sun along the entire length of the crescent-shaped city, porpoises playing their lazy, unwieldy gambols around your rather ponderous craft, women coming and going up and down the steps with *chatties* on their stately heads, and the more devout among the people praying and bathing for the second time that day; to see the pale smoke rising from this pyre and that on the shore at the foot of Manikaranika's *ghát*, and to watch the quickly consuming fires beneath,—not too quick for the demand, as many other long, narrow swathed bundles of mortality are lying with their dead feet in the holy river awaiting their turn to become ashes,—is a grim and, at the same time, a uniquely picturesque and memorable sight. When fresh kindling is required, the fire is brought—oddly enough, as the office commends itself, as a sacred one—from the house of the low-caste Domra, whose monopoly it is to supply it, and whose pocket has grown fat on the enormous fees sometimes exacted from the wealthier among the people. At the head of this most sacred of the *ghàts* is the Temple of Sarkeshwara, the "god who ferries over," a very significant rendering of his name.

As we drifted down the sweeping, rolling river, a wedding party embarked at one of the *ghâts* in a small boat to cross to Ramnagar on the opposite shore. They let out in their wake a chain of marigolds, one end of which was fastened to the landing-stage and which was long enough to reach across the Ganges. They sang, as they rowed, some festive wedding chorus, with a refrain to the effect that if the bride pleased her husband he was to give her a necklace as long as the flower-chain. Presently the song abruptly ceased, and to our sorrow we found that we had drifted across the track of the yellow chain and had snapped its frail lengths in two. Many dismayed and re-proachful glances were cast back at us, and, whatever the ultimate result might be, it was to be feared that we had unwittingly filled the little dark-eyed bride's soul with forebodings and seriously disturbed the harmony of the day's observances.

Next morning we found the scene transfigured in a bewildering manner. In the pale yellow light of the dawn the whole line of *ghâts* was alive and flashing with movement and colour. Where a dream-like stillness had reigned before all was now animation. Rajahs and beggars, *purdah* ladies and *pariah* women, alike found their level on the shores of holy Mother Gunga. Gay silken *saris* were left in the dressing sheds, and delicately nurtured ladies stepped eagerly down the steps into the foul-looking water rolling silently at their feet, drinking it and immersing themselves in it again and again, and shivering the while. So also did enfeebled old men and little children. One miserable little boy pleaded piteously for exemption after three "dips," but his father was inexorable and plunged him overhead, gasping and reluctant, even until the regulation seventh time.

But such was the prayerful abstraction of many that they appeared wholly unconscious of their chilled and benumbed condition. Young men performed strange fantastic gymnastics in the water, and cripples dragged their distorted and paralytic limbs down the *ghát* steps. Dead and dying were alike carried to the hallowed shore. To which class a little baby belonged which was flung into the sullen, rolling waters, I know not.

The little platforms shaded by monster umbrellas were now occupied by *gosains* and *fakirs* who received offerings, in return for which they gave blessings and inscribed their respective caste-marks on the foreheads of the faithful. Everywhere the sacred yellow prevailed, the poorest pilgrims among

the throng having contrived to possess themselves
of *sari* or turban of the distinctive colour, and the
broad band of ever-shifting hues which bordered
the river from end to end of the *ghâts* absolutely
glittered in the morning sunlight with gold, orange,
and salmon, with here and there a flash of green
or red, the whole tempered by copper-coloured
skins and white linen raiment.

Later in the day the same people in thousands
were to be met in the old city. In the maze of
narrow, tortuous, sunless alleys, which call themselves streets, all classes were again to be found,
from the poor and dying who, lying on their
charpoys, were waiting for death, happy in that
some good friend had dragged them to this blessed
and auspicious spot to meet him, to the Nautch
girls, those "handmaids of the gods," who paraded
their wantonness without reserve. There were
ladies too of high degree on foot. As we passed
through one of the cool, eight-foot-wide streets we
met three little Hindu ladies veiled to the eyes.
When they saw that dangerous animal, the *saheb*,
coming, they incontinently and with one accord
scrambled into a doorway and shrinkingly grouped
there with their heads together and their backs
towards us like three frightened rabbits. I glanced
back at them after passing and found them furtively
peeping sideways at us from under their *purdahs*,

speechless and motionless, till we were well out of sight.

And thus we thread our way amid the multitudes who were passing hither and thither through the labyrinthine alleys, meandering through the quaint bazaars, and hurrying from temple to temple, now to lay gorgeous piles of marigolds before Shiva's shrine, again to cast offerings of milk, sandal-wood, or *bel* tree leaves into the "Well of Knowledge," his favourite abiding-place in the court of the Golden Temple, the air of which has become rank and poisonous from the fetid accumulation of decaying vegetation. Above all they must stop before the cone-shaped *lingam* stone, the emblem of reproduction, splashed and daubed with Indian-red paint which is symbolic of the sacrificial blood of bygone days. Again, they feed Durga's sacred monkeys, or offer a garland to Shakareshwar, the giver of handsome sons. Anapurna, too, the bread-giver of Benares, must have a votive, and the frightful Ganesh, the elephant-headed god of wisdom, must not be passed over. The Hindu Pantheon is widely represented in Benares, and only when the pilgrims have accomplished their *Paneh Kose*, or ten miles circuit of the city and its shrines, can they obtain at the Temple Sakohi Vinayak, the "witnessing deity," the much coveted certificate entitling them to the spiritual privileges for which they have toiled so laboriously, and often at the expense of so much suffering and weariness.

A higher phase of Brahmanism finds its representative in Benares in the person of a holy recluse called Swamiji Bhashkaranander, who has his abiding place in the Anandbegor Garden of Happiness, near the Durga Temple. He receives with courtesy any who will visit him of either sex. Only, as he has long since divested himself of the vanity of even so much covering as a *koupin*, it is prudent to enter the holy precincts with a little stir, in order that he may have notice of your advent, and out of deference to any narrow prejudice you may have in the matter, assume that rag or semblance of decency before you approach—not that either his modesty or his dignity suffer from lack of clothing, for he is a fine example of Carlyle's theory to the contrary. He regards you with a direct and genial glance, and whilst peeling you a banana, he will tell you, through the medium of an interpreter, how, having been born under the most auspicious of astrological combinations, he had, at the age of seventeen, as it were, awaked from a dream, and had begun " to see through the unreal nature of the world," to feel "the existence of one supreme Spirit, the All-being of the Almighty throughout the universe," and to know that "true knowledge alone can enable us to realise the great Spirit." He goes on to tell you how, like Gautama Buddha, he had left his young wife and newly-born son and had gone forth to live a life of self-renunciation, worship, and study of the Shastras and Vedantic philosophy; how he had spent years of days in the contemplation of the human soul as being one with the Supreme Spirit, and had made many pilgrimages. "Visits to holy places," he says, "train the mind because the time thus employed is spent in the contemplation of the Supreme Being, and you also come across such scenery as would arouse the dullest imagination and call up in your mind thoughts of the Creator."

And so Swamiji, like saints of other times and communities, had passed, through penance and much tribulation, from one stage of sanctity to another, until he had attained to the science of Yoga, and with it a supreme indifference to the things of time. He is a very St. Francis in his rejection of lucre, and depends for his food on the charity of the people. Pundits come from afar to ask from him interpretations of difficult points in the *Shastras*, or to discuss with him their abstruse introspective Hindu philosophy, whilst others come to beg his intercession in obtaining for them the earthly blessings upon which they may have fixed their earthly hearts. Many such came while he spoke with us, and, kneeling, kissed his feet with all reverence.

It was difficult to reconcile the high - souled theories and simple practice of the *Yogee* with the scenes we had witnessed in and about the city; but he tells us that "we have so far lost our power of perception by study of Western literature and science as to be unable to see the truths of Hindu religion or to distinguish between worship by symbol and the worship of idols." Theoretically it may be as he says; but in the vulgar worship it is to be feared that the great *Para Brahm* is commonly lost sight of in the multiplicity of the Hindu Pantheon, and that the symbol has largely merged into the idol—a common danger from the days of Moses until now.

Swamiji shook us warmly by the hand at part-ing and eagerly presented us with a pamphlet containing a history of his life and an epitome of the complex religious system of the Brahmans, a strange compound of high morality, metaphysical subtleties, and gross superstition. What struck our narrow Western minds as paradoxical was the tone of extravagant panegyric concerning Swamiji himself which ran through the pamphlet, and which, for him to distribute among his visitors, hardly seemed compatible with the severe and

8

rigid self-renunciation of his profession. Possibly he and his disciples would have explained that his spiritual state reached far beyond any such puny and cramped consideration,—another dangerous conclusion. But the man was no charlatan. He firmly believed in his creed and in his own suffi- ciency. His, doubtless, was the Brahmanism of the Vedas, but was certainly not that of the people. The practice of demonolatry, the worship of blood- thirsty Kali with her "necklace of skulls" and her devilish red eyes, the filth and degradation of the Durga Temple with its bloody sacrifices, its monkey abominations, its fetid odours, and its sordid priests, were still vividly pictured in our memories, and we found it hard to accept Sir Edwin Arnold's earnest assurance that "even the poor peasant of the fields will tell you that the symbol they worship is only a symbol."

That the human soul must worship *something*, objective or subjective,—if not external to self, then self itself, in one form or another,—the evidence of the world's history goes to prove. And whilst dwelling on the comparative analogy of different religions and the nature and strength of their moral influence, no one can deny that the object of a man's worship must either dignify or degrade him. Yet, in spite of the lowest phase of Hindu rites which are practised in the name of the gods, it is universally acknowledged by those who have taken the trouble to inform themselves concerning the masses in India and their ways that they are simple, hospitable, gentle, patient, and charitable; as free from gross vices as most of European races, and excellent, if not too indulgent, parents. And as there is nothing in their religion, as it now exists and is practised, to discipline or restrain them, no interior motive to good, the outward morality, order, and decency which is to be found among them must be laid—all, at least, which does not spring from their innate patience and docility—at the door of their caste system, that stern and terrible code of Menu, any offence against which is punished promptly and severely with suspension of caste privileges, a penalty which means social and religious death, and which has, for them, far greater terrors than any remote contingency of punishment which a future life may bring. To be pursued through every phase of life with the dreaded penalties, to be unable to marry himself or to give his children in marriage, to be unable to receive so much even as a cup of cold water from any member of his family, to live under a relentless ban of disgrace and ostracism, and to die without benefit of clergy, is the fate which the loss of caste brings on a Hindu, a fate which to steer widely apart from is the leading and vital principle of action in each one of the race. The restrictions are from without and not from within the man, and the result is superficially satisfactory.

In addition to its graver and very wholesome moral laws, Menu's code teaches a careful self-restraint, even in small things, which must help to strengthen the moral nature. For instance, the train which we entered on leaving Benares was full of newly-arrived pilgrims. As the third-class carriages disgorged themselves the exhausted condition of some of the passengers was very apparent. These, it seemed, were high-caste people though poor in this world's goods; and they would never dream, if there were one Pariah, Chandula, or other low-caste Hindu in the same compartment with them, of either eating or drinking in his presence. Comfort and health would alike be sacrificed rather than they should be guilty of such infringement of caste laws. Perhaps few of the results of English administration are valued by the Indian people more than the means of reaching easily their great *trithas* or holy places afforded by the network of railway lines which is spread over the country. But many natives of high-caste still prefer to perform their pilgrimages by road rather than incur the alternative of losing caste, or of arriving at their destination exhausted and faint for lack of food which they have not had the opportunity of taking.

Again, the *pani-wallah*, who carries water in his *lota* the length of the train at each station, must always be a Brahman; otherwise parched and thirsty high-caste throats would have to remain parched and thirsty. Squalid he may be, and generally is, but the sacred white cord, like a piping cord, across the left shoulder indicates his caste and enables others such to profit by his ministrations. Those of lower caste he also succours, but they must leave their carriage and squat on the platform whilst he either pours the water from a height directly down their throats, or into the stoup which they form with one hand just under their lips, and from which they drink as quickly as the water flows into it. Empty and purposeless though such ordinances appear in themselves, it is doubtless the stringent observance of them which imparts to the Hindus the moral strength which they possess. It is the keeping of a law of obedience which is the outcome of fear, but, failing one which is higher and holier, such a law is better than none, and, well kept, surely helps to prepare the way for better things.

VIII.

AKBAR'S FOLLY.

"I AM dr-r-runk with the beauty of this place," was the ejaculation uttered in emphatic tones and guttural accent by our Austrian *camarade de voyage* a few days after he had reached Agra. And in the midst of the surpassing beauty of palaces, bridges, tombs, and mosques—the work of Hindus, though built for the Moghuls—which help to make the city glorious, it was the Taj Mahal which seemed especially to have cast a glamour over his mind, as it does over those of so many. Why, it is rather hard to say. It possesses a magical, dreamlike beauty wholly its own, and its story appeals to the sentiment and imagination, but if architecture is "poetry in stone," surely the utterances of the Taj are not those of the highest intelligence. To compare its shallow motive with the stern force and majesty of the Hindu temples would be to compare an ode of Pope's with a book of Virgil's, or a melody of Verdi's with one

of Handel's choruses. Beauty of detail it possesses
in the highest degree, but the want of unity in its
plan is disconcerting, the inharmonious arrangement of the four minarets straggling, as they do,
widely apart from the balloon-shaped dome, and
in no apparent sense belonging to the group.

Doubtless the chief beauties of the Taj are
rather accidental than intrinsic, and lie, to a great
extent, in its exquisite fabric of milk-coloured
marble and its delicious setting in the stately
garden where oriental luxuriance abounds, where
white marble pavements chequer the greenery, and
where a cool lotus-studded canal flows silently,
and as it were to worship, at the foot of the
domed monument. But all that there is to see
is seen at once. There is nothing of hidden
charm to search for. There, on the bank of the
great river, sits the Taj, radiant, dazzling, shadow-
less, like a fair white queen whose beauty fills
the eye at a first glance, but who knows no mood
other than the present. Had the tomb of Humayan,
or that of Safdar — one built nearly a century
before the Taj, the other a hundred years after it,
both on similar lines and both in Old Delhi,—had
they been of milk-coloured marble instead of stern
red sandstone, the tomb of the Crown Lady would
never have been the pre-eminent thing that it is.

Again, the story of the Taj Mahal's being, one

touching the love of man for woman, lends it another charm. Arjamund must indeed have been adorable to have been so adored, and all one's natural sympathies are enlisted in the romantic sentiment of the great Moghul, Shah Jehan, who has so triumphantly preserved from oblivion the memory of his beloved Mumtaz-i-Mahal, the "Exalted of the Palace," and the mother of his eight children. But that is another thing, and you have but to cross the Jumna to find, on the opposite shore, the tomb of Itimadu-Daulah, modest and unpretentious in size, but surely in its symmetrical lines, its harmony of composition, and its marvellous lattice-work windows there is more of pure art and of true beauty than can be found in any part of the Taj. Built in the previous reign in memory of the Persian father-in-law of the Emperor, it is a bit of pure Indo-Moresque work of perfect proportion, exquisite detail and workmanship, and delicate feeling, without any "watering-down" by Italian decorators.

But one has to go to Futtehpur-Sikri, the City of Victory, to find the most beautiful tomb in India. At the extremity of an absolutely level and nearly straight road which stretches its twenty-two miles of length westward from Agra, lie the ruins of the red and royal city which might justly be termed "Akbar's Folly,"—for even his follies

were on an illustrious scale. It is worth while
to journey along that road if only to see the birds
in their legions and of every hue and variety which
have their home in the green arcade of interwoven
boughs mercifully contrived by the continuous
rows of trees on either side of the way, and without which the portion of the traveller would be a
scorching one. Paroquets and green pigeons,
kingfishers blue and terra-cotta, flaunting jays,
aristocratic hoopoos, bee-eaters bronze and green,
kingcrows and chattering mynas go flashing their
rainbow hues in and out among the sombre trees.
Pearl-grey doves coo their mournful love-song and
larks carol gleefully to compensate for the screeching of their more showy and less gifted fellows.
Except a camel and his rider now and again, or
a party of gaily dressed, chattering natives on their
way to Agra bazaar in an *ecca*—one of the queer
jingling vehicles of this country, like a Punch and
Judy show on wheels, made of brass and canopied
with white, and upon the platform of which four
natives manage to squat comfortably—there is little
to vary the monotony of the three hours' drive.
But at the end of this long aviary, and occupying
a sandstone ridge which rises abruptly from the
level of the vast plain, you find a great red city—
a city of ruins. Piled-up remains of red sandstone
buildings on either side of the road bring forcibly

to your mind the remembrance of Pompeii, a memory which is strengthened as you advance and discover, in the midst of the devastation, treasures of art hidden away like precious ore amid rubble.

Why this city of palaces, so isolated and so strangely remote, was built, and, still more, why it was deserted, remains more or less of a mystery. The story goes, and obtains among the people, that Akbar, after the death of his two eldest sons, went in his sorrow to invoke the assistance of Salim Chisti, a holy *fakir* who lived a hermit's life in a cavern in the desolate district. The *fakir* told the emperor that not until a life had been voluntarily sacrificed for his intention would his prayer be heard and an heir to the throne born to him. Salim's son was standing by, and on hearing his father's sentence he, in Akbar's name and to propitiate Heaven, forthwith committed the happy dispatch which was to bring peace of mind and an heir to the Emperor. This was by no means an impossible or even improbable incident. The boy came of a race of so-called saints, and had lived his life in an atmosphere of religious exaltation. Sacrifice is the very essence and genius of Indian devotion, and it might seem a small thing to the son of the *fakir* to purchase for himself blessedness at the expense of a very

joyless existence here upon earth. Those were
the days of *sati*, when many a Hindu widow
—always of her own free will—laid down her life
cheerfully for the sake of her husband's soul.
And although of different race and creed, the
spirit of self-immolation belonging to the ancient
faith had, thanks to the swift sympathy and
emotionality of the East, reached Islamism as it is
in India. On the fulfilment of Salim's prediction,
Akbar, as an act of thanksgiving, built a city
which, like all his undertakings, was on the most
lavish and sumptuous of lines, near the scene of
the boy's self-sacrifice. This history of its *raison
d'être* is recounted to you eagerly and with absolute conviction by the broken-down remnant of
its population, who burrow, so to speak, in the
ruins of the city and claim descent from the saint.

But whatever the cause, the architectural result
is a very triumphant one in this the favourite
residence of the great Moghul. You realise to the
full the splendours of his court, the most gorgeous
that even gorgeous India had ever known, as you
pass from under the Naubut Khana, or great
gateway, within the crenulated walls of the Fort.
From its upper chamber bursts of martial music
used to welcome the Emperor on his arrival from
Agra, whence he would travel by that long straight
road with his retinue of courtiers, his lines of

elephants, his camel corps, and his men-at-arms.
Hardly was the great Treasury, now in ruins,
vast enough in its day to meet the needs of
Akbar's yearly revenue of £30,000,000, royally
and punctually disbursed though it was; for no
man knew what it was to be the Emperor's
creditor.

Thence you pass on to the cloistered Diwan-i-
am, measuring one hundred and eighty feet from
east to west, and more than double that from
north to south.   A hall and verandah project
into the great quadrangle at the west side,
and between the two beautiful screens of pierced
stone which form its central feature it is easy to
picture Akbar, of the race of Timour, a man of
great capacity and of noble stature, ruddy-brown
of skin, and with straight eyebrows stretching
across the broad, strong brow and meeting over
his grave, dark eyes—hearing causes, delivering
just judgments, and receiving the salutations of
his people, the form of which, *Allahu Akbar*, "God
is great," was as simple as his response, *Jalla
jallalahu*, "May His glory be glorified."

Within a stone's-throw of the Audience Hall is
Akbar's Sleeping-Room, called his *khabgar* or
House of Dreams.   Though one can hardly suppose that the few hours of sleep which he allowed
himself out of the twenty-four would be disturbed

by many dreams. This is one of the simplest chambers among the palace buildings, and stands apart from all else except the one beneath it, which was occupied by his Hindu *guru* or astrologer. From the Emperor's private room a covered way led to the Council Chamber, a curiously constructed hall with an elaborately carved central shaft, from the immense corbelled capital of which spring four stone causeways with trellised balustrades, also in stone, at either side. These little causeways radiate to the four quarters of the earth and join a gallery which runs round the chamber. The adjoining *Auk Michauli*, where you are told the great Moghul used to play " hide-and-seek " with the ladies of his zenana, would alone be sufficient to make the place artistically famous, with its windows of stone lace-work, its roofs, some coved, others supported on heavily carved struts, its graceful pilasters, and its painted ceilings.

The Emperor could also reach, without observation, by hidden passages from his own chamber, the Palace which was built by the Rajah Bir Bal for his daughter, Akbar's Hindu wife. Like the rest of the royal city, it is entirely of red sandstone and its entrance porches, its panelled and richly carved walls, its cupola'd and bracketed roofs, its sculptured friezes and corbels, its highly wrought doorways, and its latticed terraces are unique in the elaborate variety and original beauty of their design. Not one square foot of timber was used in the construction of this curious and singularly beautiful two-storeyed palace of the Hindu Queen.

Of the Sultana's House only one small pavilion now remains, thought by many to be the gem of the Palace, but which wearies the eye by its profusion of ornament. The spirit of redundancy and unrest had got the better of the artist's sense of proportion, and he has left no square inch of flat surface, not even on the soffits of the cornices nor on the under sides of the eaves which overhang the verandahs, the supporting pillars of which are dreams of gracefully conceived design. Again, all is of red sandstone. So is the Panch Mahal, or Recreation Palace of the imprisoned zenanas, a five-storeyed colonnade enclosed on all sides by screens of stone lattice-work, each tier of which, pagoda-like, is smaller than that below it, so diminishing to a mere ridge at the top. Its lowest storey is supported on fifty-six columns covered with delicately wrought tracery, no two of which are alike. In this maze the ladies of the court held their wild revels, playing hide-and-seek and blind-man's-buff. It is good to know that they ever did anything so wholesome. Akbar too had his frivolous moments, if you may judge from his *Pachisi* board, which still shows its outlines on the stone flags of one of the courts, and where history tells you that the game was played after the fashion of chess, with slave girls as "pieces" to take the moves.

The "House of Miriam" has its own tale to tell of isolation and despondency, worse than that of any "moated grange"—the story of a Portuguese Christian as one among many wives, a Nazarene among Mussulmani. Her house used to be called the *Sunabra Makan* or golden House, because of the gilding and painting which had adorned it. But little of this remains except some defaced frescoes. It seemed a strange place in which to find a picture of the Annunciation. And yet, on the exterior of the Christian girl's house are the faded remnants of a fresco clearly showing the outlines of an angel's wings, and other indications of the sacred subject which it had served to represent in the conventional mannerism of the time. Here, too, is Miriam's garden, with her bath in one angle of it, in the centre of which is the broken shaft of the fountain which would tinkle and drip its monotonous tone in her forlorn ears whilst she wandered amid the jasmine and tuberoses, and poured out her lonely soul to the listening casuerina tree, that most sympathetic thing of still life, the feathery boughs of which respond with a low sigh to the gentlest breath of a southern wind. Overlooking Miriam's garden is the south side—rich in colour and ornament—of the Palace of Rukia, the Emperor's chief wife. Truly, if finely gilded cages could make prisoned birds content, those poor ladies had nought to complain of.

At the north-west extremity of this city of dead glory, rising through the quivering air and against the dense blue Indian sky, is the *Harin Minar* or Deer Minaret, which is said to cover the burial-place of Akbar's favourite elephants, — perhaps because the tower, to its height of seventy feet, is finialed with elephants' tusks. You are told that from its summit he used to shoot black buck and other big game which was driven within range of his rifle by his *shikari* on the plains below. To reach this tower you must pass the Caravanserai, an enclosure of 250 feet square, which was the market for all the richest merchandise of the day. Akbar's court and splendour demanded contributions from every country that knew what art produce meant, and to Futtehpur-Sikri the merchantmen brought of their best and choicest.

> "Rich gifts
> In golden trays; goat-shawls and nard and jade,
> Turkises, 'evening-sky' tint, woven-webs—
> So fine twelve folds hide not a modest face—
> Waist-cloths sewn thick with pearls, and sandal wood."[1]

[1] Arnold, *Light of Asia.*

Such-like they brought from China, from Persia, and from Europe, and were always sure of a ready market and just dealings.

But the crowning glory of Futtehpur-Sikri is its mosque—said to be a reproduction of the Mecca mosque, though it is difficult to understand how its labyrinth of mighty pillars, sculptured and decorated in the characteristic and unique Hindu style, could have been borrowed from Mecca. Probably its plan of three square inner courts with zenana chambers at either end has been arranged on the lines of the Mecca mosque, but there is nothing, otherwise, in the massive beauty of the noble and ornate red sandstone architecture to suggest Byzantine influence. Enter the vast quadrangle by the *Bashahi*, or Royal Gate, and on the north side of it—hidden away like a rare gem in the heart of this great city—you find the most exquisite mausoleum that ever graced the memory of man. It courts no prominence, and the spirit of display is unknown to it. But from the marble lattice-work screens which surround it—matchless of their kind in beauty and variety, for Hindu architects rarely condescend to repeat themselves—to the brackets which support the broad eaves, the doors of ebony and brass, and the tomb itself covered with tortoiseshell and mother-o'-pearl inlay of rare artistic design, it

9

is perfect in all its parts ; and those parts go to
form a whole in the harmony of which there is
no shadow of violation. All is consistent, and,
though chaste and reserved, is perfectly articulate
and significant—a rare and holy thing of beauty,
a sonnet in marble to sing the praise, to successive
generations, of the man whom the Emperor
delighted to honour — the same Sheik Salim
Chisti who foretold the birth of his heir, and
whose reputation for sanctity was the probable
cause of the building of this city of marvels.
"May God hallow his tomb," which is the resort
especially of childless women, both Hindus and
Mussulmani, who come to ask his intercession that
their reproach may be removed.

Over against the Dargah of Salim, on the south
side of the quadrangle, is the Gate of Victory,
built by the Emperor to commemorate his victories
over the kingdoms of the south. And well worthy
is it of such an occasion, with its one hundred and
thirty feet of height and colossal proportions.
Externally, a vast flight of steps leads down from
the platform upon which the mosque is built to
the level of the plain below, a depth of thirty feet.
The immense doors are absolutely covered with
horse-shoes, votives nailed there by the owners of
sick horses, who attributed their cure to the prayers
of the saint. Within the arch on one side there

ENTRANCE TO DARGAH. FUTTEHPUR-SIKRI.

is inscribed the date of Akbar's—"The king of kings and the shadow of God"—coming to Futtehpur-Sikri, and on the other there are words of which the following is a translation:—"Isa (Jesus), on whom be peace, said, 'The world is a bridge. Pass over it but build no house on it. The world endures but an hour. Spend it in devotion.'" A high and holy precept, but one which Akbar was the last to follow.

From the summit of this monster gateway the parched and sterile plain may be seen stretching away and losing itself in the purples and greys of the horizon without trace of water anywhere, and it is easy to understand that the lack of it may have caused the unhealthful condition of things which ultimately, doubtless, drove the court away from Akbar's favourite residence, his imperial and beautiful city. In his time the water of a lake which lay to the south-west of the Deer Minaret was pumped up by Persian wheels into reservoirs on a level with the palace, and the drying up of this lake may have caused the city's doom.

Hanging from the arched roof of the gateway, like masses of black sponge, was an accumulation of wild bees' nests. The bees of India are not the negatively offensive insects which we know at home. They are twice the size of English bees with (morally) a strain of the wasp in them, and are by nature extremely aggressive. An old lady whom we knew had gone to Futtehpur, armed with her *Fergusson*, on architectural investigation severely bent. Whilst standing under the gateway she peered upwards through a pair of large field-glasses in order to master religiously the construction of the arch. This was more than the bees would stand, and presently they began to swarm down upon her and her weapon of offence, the double-barrelled glasses. They stung her hands and face, and as she fled they followed, till with a presence of mind borne of desperation she rushed into a dark recess, leaving the cloud of winged fiends outside. There she was ultimately found in such a condition that she had to be carried back to Agra in a litter. It is needless to say that we very carefully concealed our glasses whilst we were in the vicinity of the bees' nests, and satisfied ourselves with a somewhat cursory inspection of their domain.

A very dignified and obtrusive old moullah attached himself to us, and in a futile and irritating manner chanted in a croaking voice, as we went along, verses of the Koran in, to us, an unknown tongue. He was the grandfather of our guide, who continually urged upon us the fact that "he was not only a guide but a descendant in the twelfth generation from Salim the saint." Their

illustrious pedigree nevertheless did not deter
them from begging in a most abject way for
bakshish over and above the proper fee. Another
grave-looking Mussulman brought an offering of
very deadly-looking sweetmeats, and a third some
rather dashed and depressed-looking flowers, all of
which meant *bakshish.* And their courtly dignity
had something so compelling in it that remon-
strances died on one's lips, and, for the moment, we
almost felt that ours was the honour when they
accepted our rupees.

But nothing could detract from the delight of
wandering about the cloisters and gardens and
palaces of this city of ancient beauty, making new
and delightful discoveries at every turn—here a bit
of mosaic, there a hidden and rarely beautiful
window, or again, the blue tiles which sparkle
like gems over the gabled roofs of the Palace of
Rukia, the Hindu Empress whose influence over
the Moghul may perhaps be thanked for the happy
intermingling, or marriage, so to speak, of the two
styles of architecture so distinctive of his works.
And the blending of the two schools, the best
qualities of each predominating,—of the exuberant
ornament of conventionalised flowers, birds, and
animals of the nature-worshipping Hindus with
the monotonously beautiful, mathematical, interlacing lines of the iconoclastic Mohammedans,

who would suffer no portrayal of living thing to
appear in their work; the more refined and
delicate Saracenic tempering the crudeness of
the Indianesque, which, in its turn, lends force
and majesty and grandeur to the other,—produces
a style of its own which nowhere perhaps, except
in the Killa Kona Mosque at Old Delhi, finds
completer expression than it does in the ruined
and deserted city of Futtehpur-Sikri.

IX.

A NAWAB'S SHIKAR.

FROM Agra to Aligahr, and thence by Chandausi and Bareilly, we travelled through Rohilkund to the farthest limit of the railway. Through leagues of *dahl* fields covered with the yellow blossom which in harvest-time will become lentils—lentils of the sort, you are told, which, in the form of the historic "mess of pottage," cost hungry Esau his birthright,—and through acres of white poppies which covered the opium fields and stretched their snowy sheets over the land, we sped on our way to Rampur. There we arrived at midnight, to find that our baggage had been left on Chandausi platform. Travel-stained and unkempt, therefore, we had not only to present ourselves to the Resident and Mrs. Colvin, but on the following morning to receive his Highness when he came, in all the pomp of *sowars* and *syces*, to bid us welcome to his state and to ask us to dine with him that evening—an invitation which he considerately left open till we knew whether or not our missing "kit" had turned up. Even he recognised the indubitable fact that we could not dine with a Nawab without the usual appliances of social *convenances.*

Happily things fell out rightly, and with renewed self-respect and a sense of dignity born of clean linen and suitable raiment we reached the Palace, which is in the heart of the city, at eight o'clock. The courtyard was full of solemn, silent retainers. Some were smoking, others were contemplating; but none of them were apparently employed in any beyond those passive forms of occupation. A native regimental band was stationed under the dining-room windows, ready, when the guests were seated, to discourse such music as they knew. Carpets were spread across the courtyard, and we were received by a cousin of the Nawab's, a splendid young Pathan in the uniform of an English *aide-de-camp.* He led us past the Palace guard and up the wide stone stairway to the entrance. Through many rooms —·cloak-rooms, ante-chambers, and screened apartments—we passed before reaching the state drawing-room, which was furnished in European style according to the conception of an Indian prince—showily and uncomfortably. In a few minutes the Nawab joined us, and with him came the principal male members of his family and circle. In spite of his career round the world the ladies of his zenana are kept strictly *purdah*, with a seclusion known to no Mohammedan women out of India. We, of her own sex, had hoped to see the young Begum, a girl of fifteen and a wife of twelve months' standing; but the poor ladies had an early start and an arduous journey of sixteen miles before them on the morrow to the Nawab's country-house, and, in the face of such unwonted fatigue, the whole zenana had gone to bed at six o'clock.

The *mauvais quart d'heure* before the announcement of dinner was occupied in studying the contents of the only book in the room—an album containing photographs of every known member of England's Royal Family even unto the third and fourth generations, a remarkably unflattering portrait of Her Imperial Majesty looking unutterable woe from the frontispiece page. A very charming old man called Hamidassafash, uncle to the Nawab, was instructed to take me in to dinner, and to judge from his anxious and perplexed countenance, the penalty which the privilege involved was a weighty one. The table appointments and decorations, like the drawing-room, were lavish and florid European in style, and the dinner, cooked, of course, by devout Mussulmans, would have done credit to a French *chef.* In the course of the *menu*, however, two immense dishes were handed round of food which presented an unknown and mysterious appearance. " That," said the Nawab to me, "is Indian food." Feeling constrained by courtesy after this implied invitation of my host to eat of the food of his country, I helped myself sparingly to what appeared an innocent compound of rice and meat—a *pillau*, in fact. But the first morsel I tasted convicted me of rash temerity. What Becky Sharp suffered in trying to swallow a chili out of complacency to her Anglo-Indian admirer was a mere bagatelle compared with my feelings whilst wrestling with that *pillau*. The *ghee* and the garlic at last prevailed, and, though the eye of the Nawab was upon me, I furtively concealed the fragments that remained of the too savoury viand under my spoon, and thankfully saw my plate vanish over my shoulder. However, he apparently bore no ill-will, for he presently announced that he had arranged to give us a big *shikar*, and that we must therefore prolong our stay in Rampur for that reason.

This invitation we found irresistible, and on the morning of the day fixed for the shoot we left the Residency soon after dawn. For some distance we skirted the bamboo hedge which— some thirty feet in height—engirdles the city with a circumference of seven miles, unbroken except by the gates. This unique form of enclosure is not regarded with favour by the more advanced spirits of Rampur, as it effectually excludes the free circulation of fresh air from the flat-lying city; but, so far, its singular beauty has prevailed over all practical and sanitary considerations, and it still continues to imprison the impurities of the city within its massive, waving wall of pale green feathers.

An hour's drive, through the rich and well-cultivated land of Rampur State, brought us to the little shooting-box where the elephants—fifteen of them—were waiting for us. Climbing the huge side of Buktaria, and over the rail of the *howdah* on her back, seemed very suggestive of scaling Delhi fort. And hardly was there time to take breath after the accomplishment of this feat when the earth seemed to totter beneath me whilst she rose to her legs, and then to my relief I found myself surveying my friends from a lofty height above them. The *mahouts* mount their elephants by stepping on their uplifted trunks and holding the flap of each ear, when the sagacious creatures raise them till they are high enough to get astride their necks, from whence, seated on pads which are often stuffed with the fibrous nests of the weaver bird, they drive them by the mere pressure of their knees on either side of the head. The murderous-looking little implement called an *ankus*—

an iron spike with a hook on one side of it—
which they carry, is used as a goad only in rare
cases of necessity, on a small raw puncture on the
elephant's shoulder.   One too impetuous tusker
received a smart rap over the head with the *ankus*
for trumpeting, as ill-bred a proceeding on the
part of an elephant as it is in a trained horse.

Through corn-fields and by way of rough tracks
we rolled ponderously and solemnly along, and at
the end of an hour had accomplished three and a
half miles, the average speed of an elephant's pace.
Then we reached the brink of a river which,
of necessity, had to be crossed.   The elephants
plunged cautiously in and very deliberately felt
their way as they splashed through the shallows.
As the stream grew stronger and deeper, reaching
to their haunches, they curled up their trunks
and lifted their inadequate-looking tails, and, as
they forded the broad river in single file, the noise
of displaced water was like a rushing torrent.   On
reaching the jungle we were joined by a motley
assemblage of beaters, a wild-looking crew armed
with huge sticks.   Then the elephants were formed
into line, and, abreast, they began to move more
slowly than before through the thick underwood.
Coolies do the work of dogs here, but many birds
were lost for lack of a good retriever.   One of the
"guns" commented in a querulous tone on "the

strange aversion of the natives to going into the jungle," but when one remembers that the jungle is full of thorns and the native practically un-clothed, the objection seems both accountable and reasonable.

When the *mahout* cried "dug," it was the signal for what appeared to be a small earthquake. First a sinking and then an upheaval of all things followed this curt remark, as Buktaria laboured over some ditch or drain, which would have promptly brought me to my knees had I not acted on the warning and clutched spasmodically the *howdah* rail. But such incidents were quickly forgotten in the excitement of watching the game rise in front of the line, which, with the beaters, covered a stretch of eighty yards, expanding and contracting according to the nature of the ground over which we travelled, the ends of the line sometimes advancing so as to form a crescent in order to ensnare the game. It seemed to come within the margin of "life's little ironies" when fifteen colossal elephants were manœuvred to corner in and encompass the destruction of one little terrified antelope. Black buck and hares were plentiful, so also were wild pig, which, in this country, never leave the jungle, and cannot therefore be "ridden" and "stuck." Black partridge, too, were looked upon as a prize, and after breakfasting on the following morning off some of the spoil of that curiously "mixed bag," I can answer for the "blackleg" being a much nearer approach, in succulence and flavour, to our English partridge than the commoner red-legged species.

Two wolves got up from their lair and trotted sullenly on in front of the line, twitching their ears and turning now and again to take furtive observations as to the possible danger which threatened them. Captain F—— fired and missed, when they vanished like guilty things, and we saw them no more.

At two o'clock, after a ride of five hours, we halted for tiffin under the welcome shade of an oasis-like group of banyans; and an excellent tiffin it was—a *pâgul khana*, or "fool's dinner," the natives would call it—too good in fact for the interests of sport, to judge from the shooting during the ensuing three hours. At the best, to shoot standing from the back of an elephant must be very like shooting from a cockle-boat on a choppy sea, and is a form of *shikar* which necessitates a long and early training. Again, the heat between three and five o'clock was very intense and very stupefying. The Himalayas to the north-west kept themselves strictly *purdah* that afternoon, and, veiled in haze, never vouchsafed so much as a glimpse of their snows to our hot eyes. Even the "elephant folk" seemed dreadfully bored, though they did their best to make things as pleasant as possible for themselves by munching continually as they went along. The fashion in which, without stopping, they tore up clumps of coarse grass by winding their snake-like trunks around them, then, with a vigorous, methodical stroke, dashing the roots first against one foreleg and then against the other to free them from soil before lifting the *bonne bouche* to their mouths, was like a dexterous feat of legerde-main. Another conjuring trick which they per-formed was to thrust their trunks down their cavernous throats, and instantly withdrawing them charged with water, to douche first one and then the other of their monstrous sides, discharging a copious shower between their forelegs as a final *coup de grace.*

All things are relative, and no ocean-churned, heaven-sent ambrosia could ever equal the delights of the cup of tea which was awaiting us at the little bungalow which we reached at six o'clock. Mrs. Colvin's barouche, too, after nine hours on elephant-back, was like "riding on an ocean wave without being sea-sick," and the ride home through the soft cool air that came with the after-glow, through the delicious, peaty, aromatic fumes of an Indian village, past blazing gipsy fires in the

jowari and *dahl* fields, where coolies were cooking
their evening rice, meant only rest and refreshment.   Only one discordant tone jarred the
pleasant harmony, and that, curiously enough,
was the note of a bird.   During the short Indian
twilight, and whilst we were changing horses at a
half-way house, a chorus of sleepy twitterings was
going on in an adjacent thicket, but above them
all there sounded now and again an unmusical
reiteration of " brainfever, brainfever, brainfe-e-ver."
" Ah," exclaimed an Anglo-Indian of half a lifetime, " there is that hateful hot-weather bird at it
again; the first time I have heard him this year."
I suppose there is hardly an English man or woman
in India who does not detest the sound of his voice,
not because of what it is, but of what it foretells.
He is a member of the cuckoo family, but instead
of heralding the tender grace of an English summer
as his relative does at home, his reappearance only
serves to remind us of the anguish of an Indian
" hot-weather " for those who cannot get away to
the Hills.   But we soon forgot the song of the
ill-omened bird in the present joy of living, and
for birds of passage like ourselves, who sail away
before the monsoon breaks or the rains and fever
come, it is hard to realise that a life spent in this
incomparable, wonderful India is not all made up
of " cakes and ale."

ı

X.

AN AFTERNOON IN DELHI BAZAAR.

IT was Friday and the month of Ramazan, the
great fast of the Mohammedans; and on our way
to the Bazaars we turned into the Jumma Musjid
of Aurungzebe, in the hope of being in time for
the mid-day prayer gathering. We toiled up the
vast marble stairway which leads from the road
to the level of the mosque platform, and entered
by the least frequented of the three great portals.
Our bearer, by virtue of his tarboosh, gained for
us admittance to the tribune or gallery over the
gateway, which we reached by a narrow flight of
steps in the wall, and which was immediately
facing the mosque proper. From this coign of
vantage we looked down on the great quadrangle
of more than 300 feet square. The mosque itself
was already thronged with the faithful, closely
packed in lines with their backs to us, and facing
the *mihrab* or recess in the wall which indicates
the direction of Mecca, whilst others continued

10

to pour in by thousands at the two side gates.
They went first to the Tank in the centre of the
court to make their religious ablutions, and then
took their places, facing the mosque, in straight
rows, according to the prayer lines which were
marked out in mosaic on the marble pavement.
Already the cloisters running round the court were
densely packed with kneeling men, and late-comers
had to be content to pray without shelter from the
torrid mid-day sun.

Three *moullahs* were kneeling on a platform
before the *mihrab*, high enough to be visible to
the whole of the assembled multitude, and at the
stated time they commenced their prostrations.
It was a strange spectacle, those 5000 men, kneeling, bowing, and prostrating as though moved
by invisible machinery, so simultaneous was their
action. At intervals only, a great cry of "Allah"
rent the air, and though uttered by those many
thousands of voices, it might have arisen from one
throat. Truly, if sound alone could pierce the
clouds and reach high Heaven, that must have
done it. There was no other audible form of
prayer, and at the end of ten minutes they began
to drift away in masses as they had come. Very
forcibly was the "essential defect" the blot, the
cancer of Mohammed's system brought home to
one by the total absence of women from this

great religious office. Not one was to be seen
within the walls of the mosque. The men, as
are the men of Delhi generally, were strikingly
handsome and finely built, and yet one could
not but remark the sullen and forbidding expression of countenance which characterised them.
This impression might reasonably have been
attributed to prejudice borne of painful association
and terrible memories, had it not been confirmed
by one who has made India and her peoples the
study of a lifetime.

Before leaving Chandni Chauk to plunge into
the labyrinthine byways of the bazaars, we paid
a state visit to the house of that prince of
embroiderers, Manick Chand, there to be tempted
well-nigh beyond our strength by some of the most
exquisite work that ever was wrought by needle,
in designs as charming as ever entered into the
mind of man or woman. Shawls and scarfs from
Cashmere, soft as the wind, were bordered with
rich gold Delhi work. So, likewise, were table-
cloths and draperies with delicate silver tracery
and jewelled embroidery. There were elephants'
housings worth a king's ransom, and ladies' gowns
—fit only to go to court in—embellished with
elaborate designs of conventionalised birds and
flowers, often copied from the old Persian and
Indian ornament to be found in the mosques and

palaces, and in such colouring as can only be found in the glowing east.

There were daintily worked *saris* for Indian and Parsi ladies of high degree, and red crape *chuddahs* with massive gold borders, undisciplined but barbaric and splendid, for Hindu princesses. Again, there were *phulkaris*,[1] the embroidered shawls worked by the women of the north-west provinces, to be worn veil-wise over their heads. Of these, Delhi can produce some of the best, the work of the Jaht women of Rohtak, a district not far from here where those gipsies of India, supposed to be of Scythian race, abound. A distinctive feature about the genuine *phulkaris* is that their rich silk diapers are all worked upon them from the back, the pattern being regulated by counting the threads of coarse brown or blue linen upon which it is worked. Three strips are worked separately and then sown together to attain the desired width, with a lofty indifference to the accurate joining of the pattern. The colours used are invariably red, green, yellow, and white, for the simple reason that silk will not take indigo, which is the only blue dye at their command. Sometimes bits of mirror are introduced into the diaper, and invariably the *goungat*, a spot of some colour in strong contrast to the rest, conveying the idea

[1] Flower-work.

that a child had got to the silk-bag and had been trying its prentice hand on its mother's work. This intentional splash of colour, however, is to denote the spot which has to be placed over the head or fastened into the girdle.

Carpet and *dhurree* making are industries of most of the Indian gaols, and Manick Chand will show you some of those made by the Delhi prisoners. They are very good, but not equal to the work done in the Agra gaol, where any carpet can be reproduced, even the finest Persian, with its sixteen threads to the square inch, and any pattern copied, even of the most intricate mosaics to be found in the surrounding tombs and mosques. The pattern is read out, as quickly as though it were a tale, to the line of prisoners who squat behind the great upright carpet frame, by the pattern-reader, who walks rapidly up and down in front, calling to each worker, as he passes, the number of threads, "three red, two white, ten blue," etc., which he has to knot into that row.

The best of Indian wares are rarely to be bought except in the towns of their manufacture. The inlay of Moradabad, the brass work of Benares, the wood-carving of Ahmedabad, the silver work of Lucknow, and the embroidery of Delhi must all be seen at their fountain-heads to be seen in perfection. Nevertheless, Manick unearthed from

his stores some of the matchless brocades of
Benares which surpassed what we had seen even
in the city of their speciality. We hear of the
brocades of our great-grandmothers "standing
alone," but these gorgeous silken stuffs of India,
stiff with silver and gold and made to clothe
Rajahs and their Ranees, would have knocked
them into heaps.

Before Manick had utterly despoiled us we
escaped from his toils and bent our steps. into the
narrow and humbler thoroughfares of the city
bazaar, where men, squatting on the raised floors
of their open-fronted shops, were beating silver
into graceful vessels and stamping old and curious
patterns on muslins and cottons. An ivory-carver
inveigled us into his den "only to look *memsaheb*,
no need to buy," and showed us costly marvels
both in massive and delicately wrought work.
A paper cutter with blade, solid and smooth, of
unblemished cream colour, the handle fashioned
into a *howdah'd* elephant, commended itself as
within the possible limits of a poor traveller's
purse. But on learning that its cost was "only
seven hundred rupees," the hope of possessing
it promptly vanished. In the shop immediately
opposite the ivory-carvers were two men, both
absorbed, one actively, the other passively, in their
occupation. They squatted in front of each other

whilst one solemnly and silently shampoo'd the jaw of the other. A few yards to the right there sat on his carpet the professional letter-writer, busily writing at the dictation of a young, eager-looking Hindu. Whether the missive was an effusive Indian love-letter or one of instruction to his native "pleader" was a matter of conjecture.

Passing down a street of tumble-down old houses, our steps were suddenly arrested by a doorway of great beauty, a doorway which led into an ancient and squalid-looking dwelling, which was all that remained of its fifteenth century grandeur. It was divided into small, deeply-recessed panels filled in with mouldings, in the centre of each of which were carved bosses in high relief. Whilst we were sketching it the inmate of the mouldering house, a grave and stately son of Islam, came forth and, with all the sympathetic courtesy of the East, invited us to place the door at any angle most convenient to our purpose, adding that he would show us many more such, and even more beautiful doors, in the neighbouring by-ways, an undertaking which he duly performed. No such doorways had we ever seen, not even in Tunis, that city of beautiful doorways.

In the course of our wanderings we passed through the bangle bazaar. Bangles and *choories* (lacquer bracelets) are an article of considerable

commerce in a country where the poorest women
are absolutely gauntleted with them, in graduating
sizes, from wrist to elbow. Indian coolie women
go to work in the fields—even such a one as Mr.
S—— saw double-harnessed into a plough with a
donkey—wearing ornaments amounting to several
pounds in weight. Some are of silver, in which
the capital of their savings is sunk, but the bulk
are of brass, coloured glass of various hues, and
of a sort of lacquer or composition, like sealing-
wax. There is a great art, as well as a significance,
in the harmonious arrangement of the diversified
colours on the arm. Here, for instance, the band
or *chun* of silver must be introduced, or one of
black or copper gilt, to throw out the vivid rainbow hues of the rest. In selecting my set I had
to call in the aid of the vendor, a woman with
dark, luminous, tired-looking eyes, small delicate
hands, and with such calm, graceful manners as
are rarely to be met with among the women of
the West.

Though the bangle-seller was a beautiful woman,
the women of Delhi, unlike the men, are not handsome; neither is their dress picturesque. The
heavily-pleated skirts, or *peshwars*, worn by the
Hindus low on the hips and made to stand out
stiffly round the feet by means of under-flounces,
are not graceful. And still less so are the *pyjamas*,

tightened at the ankle, of the Moslem women. The veiled head is the only indication of their sex. The Mohammedan ladies, however, of high degree, who keep themselves *purdah nashin*, and on whom the vulgar gaze can never rest, wear, over their *pyjamas*, trains, open before and behind, after the fashion of the divided skirt of advanced womanhood. I am told by "one who knows" that those trains are made with seventeen "gores," their "set" costing both maker and wearer much solicitude, and that those unseen in-dwellers of gilded cages are as keenly anxious that their draperies should flow in fine lines and with the proper sweep as ever was *débutante* at Buckingham Palace.

From the bangle stores we passed on to the slipper bazaar, where a rupee or two would buy shoes with embroideries on them such as would be held cheap in England at ten times the price; caps, too, in purple and gold, green and silver, black and red, that made one sorrow over the age of smoking-caps being a thing of the past. In one shop were some curious pyramidal erections of artificial flowers and tinsel. Those, we were told, were the head-gear worn by a bridegroom. This is the marriage season in India, and even as we stood there came a procession down the street headed by the usual band of so-called musicians;

then followed a long line of *ticca garis* in single
file filled with wedding guests, and finally rode the
bridegroom preceded by a company of men bearing
trophies of flowers.   He and his horse were both
covered with gauds and finery, and he wore the
regulation head-dress, from which hung a long
gold fringe entirely veiling his face.   He was
going to fetch the bride from her father's house.
But later in the afternoon another wedding party
filed through the streets, when the bridegroom had
secured his child-wife and was carrying her in
front of him—a bundle of finery, the small dark
face and form under the swathings of which he had
not yet set eyes upon.

But the day was waning, and we had yet to see
the quaint Delhi pottery, blue and white in forms
both graceful and bizarre, the silver and jade inlay,
the unique jewellery; for Delhi is famous for its
gem cutting and setting, more curious, perhaps,
than beautiful, though some of the necklets of
pearls interwoven with sapphires or rubies in the
form of network and fringes have a grace and
character of their own.

One other thing I possessed myself of before
leaving the Bazaar, and that was a tiny phial of
the costly extract of *kuss kuss* root, which every
one in India knows owes its delicious fragrance to
a drop of the ambrosia, churned by the gods from

the ocean, having fallen on the blessed *kusa* grass. The natives, for some occult reason, put it in their ears, and Anglo-Indians love it for the sake of the perfumed breezes which pass through the moist *tatis* or hanging blinds of *kuss kuss* grass, and bring relief in the " hot weather " season.

On repassing the Jumma Musjid a flood of turbaned men was pouring down the marble steps from evening prayer. Itinerant confectioners were hurrying to meet them, carrying trayfuls of fritters and cream-cakes, wherewith to enable those who were keeping the fast, which may not be broken till sunset, to take the edge off their famished condition at the earliest possible opportunity. On one side of the gateway men were selling cocks, on the other doves and pigeons, both for gaming purposes, the cocks for fighting and the doves to be used as decoys. Kite-flying is another fruitful source of gambling in India. But the sport here is pursued on much more ingenious and elaborate lines than is the simpler form of the same pastime by our small boys at home. In a village near Agra we saw a kite contest being conducted with great skill. The kites were oval, without tails, and carried an immense length of string, the upper part of which was powdered with fine glass. The point to be gained is to get above and to windward of the adverse kite, then with a swift and skilful turn of the wrist to bring one string across the other, and so cut adrift or destroy the other kite. If the aim is missed the other side gains the advantage and in its turn swoops down and makes the attack.   Large wagers are lost and won on this apparently child-like and innocent pastime, for the passion of gambling is as deeply rooted in the Oriental nature as in that of the London stock-broker or the boom-spreading American.

XI.

GLIMPSES OF RAJPUTANA.

THE combination of cleanliness and order with extreme picturesqueness is rarely achieved, more especially in India; but the city of Jeypore is a notable example of it in its most desirable form. A mile or more of white, scorching road lies, like a strip of sandy desert, between the hotel (a title of courtesy) and the city gate; an almost featureless road we found it, except for the *fakir* who squatted under a *pepul* tree and heaped the white dust of the road over his matted hair, his heavy dull face, and his absolutely naked body, whilst an adoring circle of devotees thronged around with offerings of food, waiting till he had finished his morning toilet. A few paces farther on were two hunting *chetahs*, which, with their keeper, were being exercised. These three were likewise for the moment resting under the shadow of a widely spreading banyan. Both *chetahs* were chained and one was hooded, whilst the other sat on his haunches looking out of his yellow, cynical eyes on the passers-by,—a well-seasoned and discriminating *chetah* this, and fastidious in the choice of his sport. It is long since he relinquished humankind as unworthy of his cunning.

Fortified hills, rugged and seamed, surround three sides of the city, and crenulated walls engirdle it. As you pass through the gates from the outer barrenness, it would almost seem that you are looking into the city through rose-coloured glasses, such a warm flush suffuses the long, broken lines of buildings which run down either side of the broad, straight streets. A "city of coral," it might well be named, for its houses, with their latticed galleries and oriel windows of pierced stone, its palaces and its temples are all, stone though they be, washed over with light terra-cotta tint and frescoed in white. Such treatment is, undeniably, in direct defiance of even the most rudimentary principles of æsthetic law, and yet the *coup d'œil* of these vast pink streets, thronged with native life and colour and with the fine forms of the buildings outlined against the intense blue of the Indian sky, was a unique picture and one to compel remembrance. The Rajputana colours are red, yellow, and green—and the women let you know it; for the crimped muslin *chuddahs*, woven and dyed in their own city, in which they envelop themselves, express their patriotism in as articulate a manner as colour can do; and the streets are fringed with a blaze of it. Neither are the jaunty Rajputs of the sterner sex far behind in this respect. Their turbans, coyly drooping over one ear, are always of the gayest, and the coats of the blue-blooded ones, as they curvet and prance through the city on their mettlesome Marwar steeds, are of brocades and satins and velvets of the most sumptuous.

The *Saheb logue* do not receive the outward and visible signs of servile and unquestioning deference from Rajputs that they do from others among the natives of India. The pride of race is strong within them. There is a certain savour of independence and patronage in their bearing towards you, and though they are civil, hospitable, and kindly, you are fully aware that the poorest coolie among them holds himself to be born of better blood than you. For who but themselves can trace descent from our Lord the Sun, the universal life-giver, of whom was born Rama, the first of the Rajputs? And so there is nothing for it but to accept the situation gracefully and to bear in mind thankfully that Rajputana has been habitually loyal to British rule in spite of its regarding the dominant race *de haut en bas.*

In the meantime we have passed the Palace of the Winds, the curved and fretted storeys of which,

from the base of the façade to its cornice, were
concealed by myriads of pigeons—sacred pigeons
—who billed and cooed and sidled and dozed on
every available ledge and in every hidden recess
of the coral-pink stucco work. A royal elephant
with gorgeous housing and pendant bell came
rolling down the street, and he had no terrors for
them, but as we passed under the Palace a gun
was fired at some little distance, and with the
report there arose into the air a cloud of irides-
cence. The whole Palace front seemed to come
away and to whirl and wheel in a fluttering mass
above us ; then, the apprehension and danger past,
to sail back again and to change once more the
face of the building by clothing it in plumage,
opalesque and pearl-colour.

The Maharajah's Palace is open to all who care
to see his Printing Office, his Clock Tower, and
the great Court where hundreds of retainers
lounge about in a fashion common to the
country. In India people seem to be always well
satisfied to wait. The Palace Gardens are well
kept, where pet alligators, lying like logs of dry
timber on the mud banks of the tank, come when
they are called, to be fed with the entrails of other
creatures, a delicacy eagerly disputed by the great
turtles which swim up to try conclusions with
them. But there is more of interest in the

Maharajah's Public Gardens—the Queen's Gardens he calls them—where peacocks strut during the day and roost on the trees at night, where a native regimental band plays good music and dismisses its audience with "God save the Queen," and where there is an Albert Hall, a very artistic and well-designed building, filled with a most excellent collection of Indian art produce, antique and modern, gathered with infinite pains and wide knowledge by Dr. Heaton under the direction of the Maharajah.

This and his School of Art, where you find young Rajputs of eight having their juvenile ideas shaped and their small brown fingers trained to draw straight lines and circles, and students of all ages and grades occupied in designing and manufacturing vessels and dishes in fine brass work and enamel, are clear evidences of the Maharajah's desire, not only to preserve the matchless arts and industries of his country, but to promote their further development and raise the standard of workmanship. In no other State of Rajputana is education · so advanced as in Jeypore, and the Maharajah's College, which was opened in 1844 with 40 students, numbers now no less than 1000.

Jeypore, the capital of the Maharajah's 15,000 square miles of territory, was built only in the end of last century, upon the lines of the ancient capital

11

of Amber, which, like Futtehpur-Sikri, had been abandoned by reason of its unhealthiness, and which was left standing, forlorn and beautiful, upon the slopes which rise from the shores of a lake at the extremity of a rocky gorge in the mountains about five miles from Jeypore. The reflection of the beautiful old city in the blue waters beneath it is not more silent and lifeless than its own material self. Yet Amber's ancient splendour, its alabaster Hall of Victory, with mirrored and spangled roof, its pale cream-coloured, cool bath-rooms, its sandal-wood and ivory inlaid doors, its mosaics and marbles, are just as they were left by the hands of Man Sing's architects nearly three centuries ago. By mysterious stair-cases, so narrow and dark that they seemed to be built in the wall, and along crooked passages we were led to the Jat Mandir on the upper storey. Though no longer peopled by caged women (listless or intriguing, according to temperament), it still, "with its bright and tender colours and exquisite inlaid work, looks through arches of carved alabaster and clusters of slender pillars upon the sleeping lake and silent fountain."[1] Here are still the rows of latticed arcades and balconies, through the marble lace-work of which the poor benighted souls might, if they were so

[1] Sir E. Arnold, *India Revisited.*

minded, peer down unseen and take a bird's-eye
view of the doings in the great Court and Hall of
Victory below. That was the limit of their world ;
that, and the sounds of every-day life which reached
their ears from the valley below, the creak of the
water-wheel, the screech of the pea-fowl, and the
hum of the bazaar in the town which crept round
the shore of the lake 600 feet below them. Now
silence reigns, and the shells of the houses,
wrecked and mouldering, serve as the home of
monkeys and the haunt of pea-fowl—Rajputana's
own bird, sacred to its god of war and nearly as
ubiquitous in the land as are crows in other parts
of India. Among the remnant of humanity that
still clings to the decayed city the worship of the
horrible Kali is practised in all the integrity of its
cruelty. Traces of the morning oblation were to
be seen in the stains which marked the spot where
the sacrificial blood had been spilt. The red-eyed
goddess looked out from her darkened recess, a
typical deity of such a cult.

.　　.　　.　　.　　.　　.

That native India has no clearly defined ideas
concerning bedtime was a fact painfully forced
upon us at Ajmere, where the place of our sojourn
—I cannot call it a *rest*-house—lay between the
town on one side and the station on the other.
As the hour approached when European eyelids

commonly begin to feel symptoms of pleasant languor, the town seemed to awake to a vitality unknown to it during the daylight hours of torrid heat and scorching sunshine. The Indian native possesses the power of sleeping when he will and at the shortest notice, assisted occasionally, doubtless, by the tiny brown pellet of opium which costs so little and which brings sleep and oblivion so quickly. You may often see both men and women rolling the little pills between the palms of their hands before preparing to take their casual rest. But more frequently they sleep from sheer asphyxiation, rolled as they are, without so much as a chink being left for ventilation, from head to foot in their dirty cotton sheets, and looking, as they lie about the precincts of the station or in the shadow of trees and buildings, like mammoth chrysalis. Thus they sleep, when their occupation admits or inclination prompts, without reference to day or night. And when, in addition to this, as was the case at Ajmere, the orgies of a religious festival are in full swing, those who are within earshot and who are not of kindred spirit are to be commiserated. When the tomtoms had ceased throbbing, and the chattering, singing voices had sunk to rest from sheer exhaustion on the town side, the worshippers began to surge up to the station. Then the clamour broke out anew, as train after train of pilgrims in their multitudes were despatched through the small hours of the night. The engines might have been some of the very devils that the passengers had been trying to propitiate, so wild and prolonged and exultant were their shrieks. At last one was reduced to that pitiful state of strained awakedness which, even when an interval of quiet occcurred, obliged one to lie and wait, as Carlyle did for the crowing of the cock, in pained expectancy of the next nerve-rending noise which might occur.

During the day, however, there was very much in Ajmere to efface our nocturnal miseries. During the Indian month of March, to be 1500 feet above the level of the sea is, in itself, a joy. An early morning on the shore of beautiful Lake Ana Saugar—artificial, but looking as though it had nestled in Ajmere's valley under the shadowing Taragarh hills for all ages instead of eight cen-turies only — brought rest and refreshment. To sit in Shah Jehan's own pavilion—one of many which border the blue waters of the lake—and to watch the ways of the water-birds, the *saras*, the storks, and the pelicans, whilst the cool evening breeze came sweeping down the gorge and across the face of the water to us, brought compensation for many woes.

Through a very dirty and stifling bazaar we

had to pass in order to reach the *Arkai-diu-ka-jhompra*, the " House of two and a half days," as the name signifies, that being the time occupied, according to Moslem tradition, in building the Temple. Taking into consideration that its roof is supported on four rows of eighteen columns in each, that it has a screen of seven arches, the centre of which rises to a height of fifty-six feet, most elaborately wrought and beautified with Saracenic ornament, it would require a very big act of faith, even for a son of Islam, to accept this legend. The pillars, covered with Hindu carving, are another example of the fashion in which the holy and beautiful things of the Jains were wrested from them by their Moslem conquerors to be turned to their own religious purposes. But the interweaving of the delicately outlined Kufic and Tughra inscriptions with the tracery on the fan of the arches is purely Mohammedan in style and was reminiscent of Altamsh's other great work of demolition and restoration, the Kutb Mosque at Old Delhi, where an Arabic inscription in the courtyard tells you that its materials were gathered from twenty-seven idolatrous temples.

In the heart of this same disreputable bazaar lies the chief feature of Ajmere and its centre of sanctity, the Dargah. Not until we had visited it did we realise to the full the significance of the pandemonium at which it had been our fate, so much against our will, to assist during our first night in Ajmere. Architecturally, this temple possesses no interest, but its associations and traditions are ancient and curious, and its great sanctity lies in its being the burial-place of a saint of the Chisti family. Within the great courtyard there stand two enormous cauldrons. To fill the larger of the two with rice, raisins, sugar, etc., costs 1000 rupees, and it is the custom, at their great annual festival, when some 20,000 people come to do *puja* at the shrine, for some rich pilgrim to make this offering. Fire is made beneath the cauldron, and when the food is cooked it is scrambled for by the people, eight large jars having first been reserved for strangers to the city. The men of Indracot have had the privilege from time immemorial of jumping into the cauldron when nearly empty and of scraping it clean. They are swathed to the eyes before tumbling pell-mell into the *deg*. So also are all those who take part in the distribution of the boiling pudding. But that does not prevent them getting badly burnt occasionally, and it is an article of faith at the Dargah that it is only through the good offices of Chisti that no lives have been lost.

.   .   .   .   .   .

We reached Chitor at midnight, and had to find our way to the *dâk* bungalow under a drenching, tropical rain. When we reached the desolate-looking little building there were no signs of life either in or around it. No amount of clamour on our part produced any response, but in the end Kassim penetrated to an outbuilding in the back regions and unearthed a very dazed and dejected *khansaman*, who had apparently forgotten all about us, and had rolled himself in his cotton sheet for the night. Even then our difficulties were by no means overcome, for the sole occupant of the bungalow had, for some subtle reason best known to himself, locked not only his own room door but all the other doors on the inside, and had then retired, to sink into so profound a sleep that we almost despaired of reaching his consciousness. At last our prolonged hammering—and we stood not upon the order of our hammering—produced an uncertain and groping sound, and we were relieved to see, through the *tati* behind which a night-light burnt, a pyjama'd form move stealthily, and furtively unlock first his own door and then that behind which we were shivering and bursting with all uncharitableness. Before we could push it open the pyjamas had retreated as hastily as they had advanced, and the owner thereof had vanished next morning before we were to the fore.

The little *dâk* bungalow at Chitor, or Chitargah, which belongs to the Maharana of Oodeypur, sits alone in the centre of a drear and arid plain. Volcanic mounds rise here and there within range of sight, and, at a distance of about two miles, an isolated, rocky ridge, three miles in length, rears itself five hundred feet above the level plain. The fort and ruined city of Chitor, the ancient capital of Merwar, crown its heights, and are conspicuous for miles around in this flat and featureless country.

The Resident at Oodeypur having kindly made the necessary arrangements for us, we drove from the bungalow in the early morning and were met by one of the Maharana's elephants, whose task it was to carry us to the top of the hill. He and his "people" were waiting for us on this side of the massive, ten-arched, old bridge of grey limestone which crosses the Ahr river about a mile from the city, and which has been there since the end of the thirteenth century. In its palmy days of old, when the towers and gateways at either end (now swept away) were filled with Rajput warriors and defended *à outrance*, many a mighty contest was fought out between one side of the river and the other—indeed, the very Rana who built it, Lakshman, was slain there, together with his son, when Alaudin laid siege to his city in 1303.

Hundreds of the Emperor's war elephants would trample it in the days of its youth and vigour, whereas now, the peaceable monster who was bearing me on its back, probably with little consciousness of his burthen, and whose sole aim seemed to be centred in tearing down and consuming as many banyan branches as came within the sweep of his trunk as he passed along, had to cross the river by the ford because of his weight. In midstream he stopped to douche himself, and a herd of buffaloes that were coming from the opposite shore incontinently turned and fled.

At the foot of the ridge and creeping up it, is the Lower Town of Chitor, merely a conglomeration of bazaars and narrow alleys of huts so low that in my *howdah* I found myself on a level with the roofs. We passed through the first of the seven gateways which defend the fort, the guard-room of which was full of the Rana's soldiers. And then began a toilsome, zigzag ascent up the rocky side of the ridge under a burning, blinding sun, early morning though it was. The *mahout* sang *sotto voce* quavering Hindu ditties, and the gentle-mannered, kindly people greeted us with smiles and salaams, seeing that we came under the auspices of their Rana.

Old men sat at their doors telling their beads which were made of *jiwapot* seeds, and women were spinning dreamily. A camel came grunting and snarling up the winding street, seriously aggrieved at his load of *sunul* cotton, of which he carried a fair share of bales. The gods were countless and diversified. At each turn of the road and under every *pepul* tree there was en-shrined either a *lingam*, a cone-shaped stone, the emblem of reproduction, or the memorial-stone of some hero whose spirit and memory are worshipped through the medium of this his *chattrie*. Both they and the *lingams* were splashed with red paint, symbolic of the sacrificial blood which in earlier ages would have expressed the devotion of the worshippers. Bits of tinsel, too, seemed a favourite form of offering; so also were marigolds and Shiva's *datura*. One stone, showing an open hand on it, recorded that a *sati* had been consum-mated there in 1468. A further witness to what is not generally understood—viz., that the performance of *sati* was the exception and not the rule, and was regarded as an act of sanctifying heroism on the part of the woman, who, to obtain for her dead husband a speedy remission of sin, made repara-tion for him by voluntarily sacrificing her own life on his funeral pyre. Then she who, according to the teaching of Brahmanism, could otherwise only wipe out the stain of her womanhood by marriage and maternity was besought to lay her hand on those whom she passed, and who believed that in her touch lay healing and blessing.

Through the seventh and last gate we passed, the great Ram Pol, with its inner courts and tapering pillars. Then one more turn and another short, steep ascent brought us to the platform on the top of the ridge and to the site of the ancient city, now a scene of ruined beauty.

Chitor was doubtless a great stronghold of the Jains from their earliest development, from the fact that the wonderful Tower of Fame, built in the end of the ninth century by Rana Alluji, and by far the most interesting of the surviving monuments, was dedicated by him to Adnath, the first of the Jaina Tirthankars or gods. (*We* should call them saints.) Seven carved and elaborate storeys make up its height of eighty feet; and nothing, perhaps, is more suggestive of its extreme age than the trees which are flourishing in the topmost tier, the roots of which are protected by the accumulated dust of ages, and must find their nourishment in the chinks and joints of the ancient masonry. Near the Tower of Fame were the ruins of a very exquisite little temple full of the delicate, graceful carving so characteristic of Jaina architecture. A colony of flying foxes were in residence here, and were hanging in hundreds from every available point

TOWER OF FAME, CHITOR.

to which they could hook themselves in the sculptured domes.

Almost within a stone's throw of the Jaina Tower is another, the Jaya-Stambh or Tower of Victory, six centuries later in date and purely Hindu in style, of which Mr. Fergusson writes: " It is a Pillar of Victory like that of Trajan at Rome, but of infinitely better taste as an architectural object."

Rana Kumbo, who brought low his hereditary foe the King of Malwar in 1439, gave utterance to his triumph in this glorious, architectural monument, which speaks to its purpose in every line of its sculptured loftiness. An over exuberance is its fault, a fault which may be laid at the door of its style generally. But its builder, Rana Kumbo, was an artist as well as a warrior and conqueror, as may be gathered from his Palace overlooking the great Tanks, and which, four centuries old though it be, with its graceful and delicate detail and its bands of blue tiles, like turquoises and sapphires set in ivory, sparkling and vivid as on the day they were placed there, gives the world of to-day an insight into the taste in domestic architecture of Rajputana in the fifteenth century.

At that period the Jaina had given place to the Brahmanic religion, which brought, in the train of its renasence, a more careful artistic treatment of things civil than the Jains usually bestowed on any buildings except their temples. And yet the stamp of their greater refinement and delicacy of taste remained, and their chastening influence is obvious in the absence of the coarse grotesquery of the Hindu school.

This individuality of touch it is which gives such charm and vitality to Indian architecture. There is a meaning and intention in its every stone, and rarely is there a building, small or great, which has not impressed upon it the individual feeling and purpose of the builder, his race and his faith. Indians think only of the building upon which they are occupied and how best to make it fitting to its end, without thought of copy, adaptation, or "rotatory reproduction." This, surely, is the true first principle of art, and the following of which has gained for Indian buildings, past and present, the commendation of those in high authority,—of one, especially, whose criticism probably has weight possessed by none other, and who writes: "For certain qualities Indian buildings are unrivalled. They display an exuberance of fancy, a lavishness of labour, and an elaboration of detail to be found nowhere else." And again, "Architecture in India is still a living art, practised on the principles which caused its wonderful development in Europe in the twelfth and thirteenth centuries ; and there consequently, and there alone, the student of architecture has a chance of seeing the real principles of the art in action."[1]

Such is the final utterance of a "master"—that the students of his craft, to rid themselves of nineteenth century insimplicity, must turn to the natives of India and learn from them wherein lies the secret of their own decadent tendencies. The impulse of one is vital and organic, whilst that of the other is too often merely a borrowed motive, which, no matter how honourable in its primitive creation, lacks, in its second-hand, borrowed form, the spark of life and vigour, and speaks only of mental inertia and decivilised art. In one case there is a speaking face, in the other a dead mask.

[1] Fergusson, *History of Architecture.*

XII.

A PEARL AMONG CITIES.

In the days of the century's youth a drive of seventy-two miles would surely be regarded as a mere bagatelle, a summer day's pastime. But these are degenerate times, and for the moment we hesitated—only for the moment though; for not to see Oodeypur, "the city of the sunrise," would be not to see India, and our desire after her beauty prevailed. From Chitor, therefore, soon after sunrise, we started in a carriage which had been sent from Oodeypur the previous day, carrying with us our bedding and merely such other personal effects as we, being English-born, could in nowise dispense with.

The viciousness and mis-stitchedness of Indian *dâk*, or post-horses, is only a matter of degree, and to get them to start from each succeeding stage is always a question of more or less time and persuasion. At Chitor our team were abnormally fractious and stubbornly resisted all the blandishments and beguiling arguments of their driver, who, in tones of earnest entreaty, exhorted "his brothers, for the sake of the gods, to proceed," at the same time begging them to "take time to eat their breath if they so wished." But as the sole result of this affectionate appeal was a determined attempt, on the part of the team, to back us into the nearest ditch, their long-suffering relation lost his patience and began to kick them in the stomach and to heap upon their female forbears measureless abuse for instrumentally causing the being of such sons of perversity. Suddenly, without "rhyme or reason," they darted forward, and then for many miles we went like the wind over an expanse of the wildest and wastest of country, a low sage-coloured brushwood covering the ground as far as the eye could reach. Ridges of rock and mounds of volcanic outline rose on this side and that, and acacia trees, isolated or in clumps, alone relieved the barrenness of the land. A kite was busily picking the bones of a lately departed camel, whilst a company of vultures, already gorged, perched on a rock hard by and looked on placidly. The moan of the pink-crested ring-dove, the wail of the plover, and the occasional screech of a pea-fowl (Rajaputana's own bird) were the only sounds we heard until the jingle of bells announced the approach of Her Majesty's mail embodied in

12

two native runners, the man in front carrying the mail-bag suspended on a stick with a bunch of bells at the end of it, his companion following closely at his heels armed with a drawn sword, the former to scare wild beasts and the latter to be used against possible attacks by the evilly-disposed of humankind. Both seemed very inadequate means of defence. A colony of *saras*[1] stalked pompously in the neighbourhood of a small blue lake, and squirrels, striped black and yellow, scudded hither and thither among the rocks. Other signs of life there were none, except an occasional flock of emaciated goats with their herdsmen, and now and again a line of supercilious-looking camels, some snarling and grimacing under heavy loads of merchandise, others carrying armed men in pairs in the double saddles common to this country.

As we approached the first *dâk*, about twelve miles from Chitor, a cloud of dust and the sound of trampling hoofs overtook us, and we drew up by the side of the road to allow the Maha Rana of Oodeypur, the highest born of the Rajput chiefs, to pass with his bodyguard of *khaki*-clothed sepoys. His Highness, a handsome man, clothed in purple and fine linen, is believed by all orthodox Rajputs to be a direct descendant from

[1] Red-headed cranes.

Rama, whose father was the sun. His family is the eldest branch of the *Suryavansa*, or Children of the Sun, and its members have, from all time, disdainfully refused to ally their blue blood in marriage with even the mightiest of the Moghuls. The common herd of people outside the wonder-world of Rajputana may be pardoned for holding the opinion that the Maha Rana and his people probably belong to a race of Sagas, or White Huns, who overran Western India some two thousand years ago, and whose descendants are known in the present day as Rajputs. The Maha Rana was on his way back to his palace at Oodeypur with his *shikari*, camp-bearers, and other retainers, after a successful tiger-shoot at Chitor.

Near the scattered hamlets of mud huts through which we passed were patches of corn, castor-oil plants, and grain, showing vividly green in their desert frame-work, and bearing evidence that the land was capable of better things than the parched, sterile face of the plain would have led one to suppose. And about twenty miles from Chitor we entered the region of the opium farms, through leagues of which we passed—a veritable "poppy-land," only the poppies were pink, mauve, and white, never red. Opium-growing is one of the chief industries of Meywar, and what the more

inveterate of the anti-opium agitators might have
said to the radiant, fair-faced wickedness of the
land one hardly liked to think.   For ourselves, we
took unstinted delight in its beauty.   Then for
forty miles of the way nothing could exceed the
monotony of the country.   Groups of oblong
monoliths were stuck endways in the soil by the
roadside, and the splashes of red paint with which
they were bedaubed were evidence of their being
objects of worship.   Villagers we met tramping
from one hamlet to another, the men carrying only
their ineffectual-looking swords, and the women,
clothed in *saris* of indigo blue and Indian red,
invariably bearing whatever burthen there might
be to carry.   These " daughters of the sun," even
the squalidest of them, are by way of being even
more reserved and exclusive than other Hindu
women of their class, and those whom we met
always went through the form of veiling their
faces, taking care, however, to leave one eye
available, of which they made exhaustive use.
Sometimes they drove before them haggard and
careworn-looking buffaloes, beasts with an expression of well-nigh human misery stamped upon
their woful countenances.

When within eight miles of Oodeypur we
emerged from the jungle, and reached the mouth
of a valley shut in by ranges of craggy hills on

either side. Down the face of each range were built crenulated and bastioned walls which met at the base to be united by a great gateway which shut in the valley. A world of mystery seemed to lie beyond these walls, and as we passed under the heavily corbelled Hathi Pol, or Elephant Gate, the spiked doors of which stood open, we felt prepared for any marvels which might disclose themselves beyond. By degrees the jungle-clad hills lowered, and unfolded to the left of us a lake set in their midst like a gleaming sapphire. Then, still in the distance, at the extremity of the gorge, under the shadow of and against the warm, black velvet background of the farthest range, we saw a city which lay piled up in the valley, a city of white palaces and with bastioned walls, so supremely fair that it seemed more like a dream of enchantment than anything real.

At the last stage we had been promoted to four horses, and we sped through the outlying by-ways of the city at full gallop, and (it seemed) to the extreme peril of native life. At the door of the little *dâk* bungalow we were received by the *khansaman* and a sepoy policeman who had been told off to do our behests during our stay in Oodeypur. A courteous intimation also awaited us from the Dewan Saheb that one of His Highness's carriages would be placed at our disposal

whenever we wished it, an offer which we made
haste to accept. Accordingly, on the following
morning a barouche and cream-coloured horses,
together with a magnificent being bearing *two*
scarlet-sheathed swords, came to carry us whither-
soever we listed. Indeed, the fashion in which
the Maha-Rajahs of Rajputana make you free, as
it were, of their cities, and place at your disposal
their carriages, their elephants, their boats, and
their servants, is more than princely.

The grace and loveliness of Oodeypur is hard
to describe. Why did not Sir Edwin Arnold visit
it and tell the world in his vivid word-painting of
this fairest of cities? From the bazaars in the
town under their quaint arcades with corbelled
pillars, to the palaces themselves, enthroned on
the crest of their own ridge, with the intervening
Temple of Jagarnath, — rich in its frieze of
elephants and its sculptured scrolls in bas-relief,
—you find a succession of pictures full of noble
outlines and harmonious grouping. Before reaching the Bari Pol, or outer Great Gateway, you
see from the lower ground, through it and beyond
it, the Trifolia, a three-arched screen forming a
second or minor gateway to the palace courtyard.
A sculptured gallery raised on carved pillars runs
from one gateway to the other, whence the Ranas,
on sundry auspicious occasions, distribute alms—

their own weight in rupees, perhaps—to the people of the city. In the tower on one side of the gateway reposes the big gong, and in that on the other the state drums. The very mention of them is enough to set European nerves quivering.

The sepoy guard saluted the symbol of the British Raj embodied in the red-coated *chuprassie*, who had come from the Residency to look after us, as we drove into the great quadrangular court or terrace which runs the entire length of the palaces, and which is one of the noblest features in the pile. The platform on the terrace side is supported on a triple row of arches forming a retaining wall fifty feet in depth and dropping from the ridge into the valley below. Elephants, tethered by heavy chains in pickets at respectful distance from each other along the terrace, for very boredom were idly swaying their mighty bodies from side to side, and tossing over their heads and shoulders the hay which they ought to have eaten. The palace, or palaces—for each Rana adds his own, or at least a portion of one,—rise on the other side of the terrace sheer from the lake, a sumptuous pile of milk-white *shunam* in broken outlines of turrets, oriel windows, latticed galleries, palisades and *kiosks*, in a wealth of fine conception and delicate work. A very happy and artistic feature in this creation is the massive

breadth and simplicity of the lower storeys, which,
except for narrow slits, are mere stretches of
windowless wall, the buildings gradually working
up and bursting forth into richly-wrought ornament towards the roofs.   Much of the work may
fairly be compared to lace-work in marble both
in fabric and colour, for all is milk-white except
the pavilions on the topmost storey, which are
coated in Chinese tiles, blue, white, and gold, and
which sparkle like gems in their *shunam* setting.
On the palace roof there are gardens, beds of
flowers formed into geometrical patterns and enclosed in marble copings.   Water channels form
the groundwork, as it were, of the figures, and
narrow marble footways traverse them here and
there.   From these roof-gardens the view over
Pechola Lake, with its island-palaces rising like
magical creations from its blue depths, in the
waters of which every line of them is repeated,
backed by the dark-green, velvet-clad hills, is a
vision of beauty never to be forgotten.

Fateh Lal, the son of the Prime Minister, an
unusually handsome young Rajput, clad in white
satin and wearing a yellow turban and immense
ear-rings, led us conscientiously up and down dark,
narrow, mysterious stairways, and in and out of
doorways, — which were never constructed for
people of British stature,—some of carved *shesham*

and sandalwood, others of silver-inlaid ivory; from a court where peacocks blazed their plumage on the walls in glass mosaic, to the Palace of Rubies, where the same curious method of glazing and inlaying, adopted from the Persians, is used as mural decoration. The idea is a spurious and meretricious one, but the designs are so charming and the colouring is so reserved and harmonious that the effect rarely fails to please. Perhaps the best example of it is to be seen in a court and pavilion near the Pearl Palace, where the inlay of mirror on a plaster ground is like fine embroidery in silver and white.

Among the Dutch tiles which line a recess in a room of the same palace, the rest of the walls being covered both inside and out with tiles of Chinese porcelain, we discovered one bearing a picture of "The Flight into Egypt." An incongruous place, it seemed, wherein to find "The Holy Three."

The Bari Mahal, bearing upon its work the stamp of the seventeenth century, is, perhaps, with its terraced gardens surrounded by stately pavilions in pierced marble, the gem of the range ; whilst the blot in this scene of unique beauty is the palace which was built in the reign of the late Maha Rana's predecessor by an Englishman whose name it is kinder to forget than to remember, and who, as Fateh Lal gravely remarks, "when all was done, should have been tenderly dropped into the lake at the foot of its walls." This note of discord was further accentuated on entering the villa,—and enter it you must out of deference to the great pride taken in it by the Rana,—to find it furnished in Indo-European style, all velvet and cut glass, even to the gorgeous state bedstead, which is, indeed, a triumph of Mr. Osler's art. Vases of dirty artificial flowers decorated the dining-room, so incongruous as to be laughable; and yet, how vexatious that men of the same race as those who created Oodeypur should so have fallen from their high estate,—and that, alas, through "the mischievous influence of British taste." The same inartistic vagaries are very noticeable also in Japan, but perhaps, because the art of India is so stupendous, so matchless, and so supreme, such inequalities strike one with greater force here. We turned for solace to the marble terrace which "gives" on the lake and mountains, and here Fateh Lal left us to our contemplations and our photography in order to take part in the great Hindu festival, which, to the destruction of one's rest, is dragging its appalling lengths of tomtoms, *Holi* fires, processions and disorders through these many nights and days.

In the later hours of a radiant afternoon, Mrs.
Wyllie carried us off to the other side of the lake.
Our road lay through the State Gardens, where
tigers were royally pampered and petted, and
under the avenues of mango trees which filled the
air with the fragrance of their blossom. And so
we skirted the lake to the Palace of Khas Odi,
one of the many shooting-boxes of the Rana, who,
like most good Rajputs, is a keen sportsman.
From a terrace which overlooked a wide expanse
of forest and hill the *shikari* were uttering weird
unearthly cries to call the wild pig from the jungle
to be fed. The penetrating cry brought them in
hundreds into the valley below to munch the peas
which were thrown from sacks over the parapet
from a height of some fifty feet. The young ones
came greedily and incontinently. Their sires
were more wary, and slunk from cover to cover
in order to reach the banquet, keeping their
weather eye open the while in case of mis-
adventure ; whilst some surly old monsters never
left the fringe of the jungle at all, but stood
blinking viciously at the unwonted apparition of
white parasols above them. The *chakurs*, a
species of partridge, which came to share the spoil,
instead of having their heads snapped off as
might have been looked for, were treated with
great forbearance, not to say deference, by the huge

ungainly brutes. Hard by is an enclosure where
the mediævalism of India still prevails in the death
fights which take place there periodically, for the
Maha Rana's pastime, between tigers and boars.
Native manners and customs still hold sway in
Rajputana.

A rocky footpath leads from Khas Odi through
a thicket to the shore of the lake, and there we
found one of the Maha Rana's boats awaiting
us. (A *lahk* of rupees could not *hire* a boat in this
exclusive and autocratic principality.) And in it
we were rowed over Pechola's blue water to what
looked like a group of floating palaces, but which
was really the island Jagmandir. We stepped
straight from the boat on to the marble piazza,
and, in the midst of stately gardens and labyrinthine
courts and terraces, we found the Gul Mahal, or
Domed Pavilion, built erstwhiles by the Rana
Khurna for the royal refugee Prince Khurrum,
who had fled from the just wrath of his father
Jehangeer, and who was afterwards the Emperor
Shah Jehan, the builder of the Taj. His seat of
state still remains; so, also, does his mosque,
built by the tolerant Hindus for the convenience of
their guest. Some of the interior walls are enriched
by mosaics in jasper, agate, and onyx, notable even
in gorgeous India. But what appealed more to
our sympathy was the fact that, in this same

Palace of Jagmandir, sanctuary had been afforded
to many Europeans during the dark months of the
Indian Mutiny by the Rana of that day, Saurup
Sing, who lodged and entertained them royally
and loyally. Among some pictures of little account
which hung on the walls of an upper room was
one, a portrait of Saurup Sing, clearly the work of
an English hand, and a woman's. It is believed
to have been painted by a lady, one of his refugee
guests; and to us it seemed a link which helped
us to realise some of the circumstances of their
isolation and the insecurity of their lives.

Row farther down Pechola, and fifteen minutes
brings you to another island, borne upon the backs
of elephants in stone, with marble arcades and
colonnades running round its margin. This is
Jugnawas; and the palace which covers the island,
with its clustering domes and pinnacles, is the
summer residence of the Rana, who *says* there are
no mosquitoes there. The prisoned ladies of his
zenana will surely revel, if they are allowed, in the
cool gardens of the Dhala Mahal, or White Palace,
where we plucked the perfumed oleander, and
where the reservoir has been converted into a
lotus pond with flower-beds in geometric patterns
sunk in the water within marble ridges. Palm-
trees and cypresses shadow the narrow footways,
and an old Persian water-wheel drones an ancient

lay at stated times and seasons. The pomegranates are a blaze of blossom, and the air is
heavy with the luscious fragrance of the orange-
flower. The *zenanas* will find a goodly harvest
of both when the time of their summer sojourn
arrives. Another garden has walls covered with
glass mosaic in old and quaint arabesques in refined
and excellent taste.

The mountains began to put on their sable garb
as the sun sank gorgeously behind them, but one
level shaft of light still filtered through the marble
lacework of the palace's pierced windows, illum-
inating the inner recesses and disclosing more
marvels of eastern art. One room, especially, was
curious and interesting, its walls being frescoed
with portraits of favourite and notable dancing-
girls of Oodeypur. Beautiful they certainly were
not, from a European standpoint, but the ideal of
beauty being a thing so purely subjective, one can
readily understand that theirs may be the type
which finds favour in the eyes of Rajahs and their
courtiers.

From the cool shadow of the palace gardens we
watched for some time the vagaries of some ugly
snake-birds, creatures which, by a strange freak of
nature, are endowed with the bodies, malformed
and uncouth, of birds, and the necks and heads,
so far as outline is concerned, of snakes. When

swimming, the body of the bird is entirely submerged, and the long serpentine neck and head
alone are visible, rearing themselves above the
surface of the water, and giving the impression
that an aquatic reptile is moving rapidly along.
These fantastic birds suggested some creation of
"wonderland," and were very much in character
with the unreal, dream-like beauty of the scene.
Indeed, it will be long before we forget that night on
Pechola lake; for the starlight had come, and,
banishing from our minds the unworthy dread of
to-morrow's neuralgia, we still lingered under the
heights of the range of pearl-coloured palaces
which rose sheer from the water, their domes and
turrets gleaming under the white light of the
Indian moon, which had silvered the *ghâts* and
temples along the shore and pictured itself in
rippling beauty on the face of the water. Never
again on this earth are we likely to look upon a
scene so strangely romantic and so uniquely lovely.
How long it will retain its poetic and exclusive
character in the face of the railway which, in spite
of the Rana's opposition, is being laid from Chitor,
remains to be seen.

.   .   .   .   .   .

The Ranas of Oodeypur bury themselves, or
rather their ashes, in a right regal fashion. If,
as is commonly believed by those who know, the

Rajputs are of Scythian race, it would almost
seem as though the tomb-building propensities of
their Tartar progenitors had, after a lapse of more
than a decade of centuries, and in spite of their
religious teaching, reasserted themselves. Hindus,
with their undying belief in re-incarnation, presumably attach small importance to their mortal
remains. Their palaces, indeed, are regarded as
their monuments. And yet, throughout Rajputana,
many interesting mausoleums, callad *chattries*,
are to be found covering the spots where
dead Rajahs had been cremated. The finest
among them is the group at Ahar, three miles
from Oodeypur, where the remains of a remotely
ancient city still exist. A masonry wall of great
height encloses the stately tombs, which are merely
domes of graceful outline resting on pillars and ·
raised by steps some height from the ground.
They are all of white marble from the quarries of
Ragnugar in Merwar, and the beauty of their proportions and richness of their detail is very great.
The irony of things had prompted a colony of
large white-haired monkeys to establish themselves in the great mango-trees which roofed in
the enclosure. The branches were peopled by
them, and as they sat gravely swinging their
long tails or leaping from bough to bough,—
sometimes an old mother ape with her young

hanging round her neck,—their antics and gro-
tesqueries were in strange contrast to the solemn
pomp of the dead Rana's tombs, of which they had
apparently taken possession.

Not very unlike those monkeys in feature were
a party of Bheils whom we met on our way back.
The hilly tracts of Southern Meywar are largely
peopled by them. One of the original tribes of
India, they live in isolated huts, and are quite distinct
in type from their dominating superseders. Small,
black, good-natured-looking little beings, they are
pleasant to deal with except when their grim and
gloomy religion, and their faith in the supremacy
of evil spirits, whom they continually propitiate,
gets them into trouble. One of their horrible
practices, that of witch-swinging, British rule has
insistently tried to stamp out and punish rigorously
when the perpetrators could be discovered—a hard
thing to achieve. The suspected witch is suspended by the heels from a tree and swung violently
to and fro, head downward. When life is tenacious,
and the patience of the operators too sorely tried,
a stone is placed in such a position that the head
of the poor wretch dashes against it at each swing,
and so speedily terminates her tortures. It is hard
to believe that within two centuries, or even less,
similar atrocities were committed by the people of
our own civilised land.

13

But this is to talk of the seamy side of things, and one loves not, even in thought, to dwell upon aught which can cast a shadow on the memory of Oodeypur, that city of ineffable beauty set in a land of romance and poetic tradition, and peopled by a race at once chivalrous, loyal, dignified, and, in spite of the thick veneer of superstition and idol-worship, simple, patient, long-suffering, and God-fearing.

XIII.

DILWARRA AND THE JAINS.

To institute an exact comparison between the great temples of the Tamul South, where opulent splendour runs riot, and where " all that is wild in human faith, or warm in human feeling, is found portrayed " with the delicate, artistic refinement of the Jaina temples of Guzerat and Mysore, would demand the keen apprehension and architectural instinct—born of life-long study and knowledge, wide and deep—of a Fergusson. But to a mere tyro in such things the contrast of styles is most suggestive and significant, as representing another range of taste and feelings, and as expressing the artistic aspirations of another race.

Of the same religion,—for Jainaism is merely a phase of Brahmanism,—the Jains have produced buildings of rare beauty both of form and detail. From the tenth to the fourteenth century, during the wane of Indian Buddhism, was the period of their renascence and pre-eminence, religious and artistic; and though their monuments are scattered throughout Western India, and even, in a fragmentary form, in the south, the most perfect examples of their style are to be found in the clustered temples of Dilwarra, which crown the granite mount of Abu in Guzerat.

A journey of ten hot, penitential hours brought us from Ajmere to Abu Road Station, where we found that the only means of reaching Abu, a distance of eighteen miles from station to hostel, was on pony-back or by rickshaw. Furthermore, that the Holi festival being in full swing, very few coolies were available, most of their class being overcome either by devotion or strong drink. A small and inadequate staff, however, was got together. They came straight from doing *puja* to Krishna, their bodies and raiment (very limited) splashed and stained red with *gulal.* The sight of the rickshaw carried me back to the Flowery Land, a dream speedily dispelled on surveying the lank limbs of my team, which could in no wise compare with the stout understandings of the sons of Nikko; and instead of rattling gaily along at the jaunty jog-trot of the " Japs," the pace of the five "human cattle" who propelled me never exceeded a walk during the eighteen miles which dragged their weary lengths over seven hours.

Happy, good-natured, and civil, the men sang

snatches of quavering Hindu melodies, perspired
freely, till the *gulal* trickled down their black skins
in small blood-red streams, and chattered and
laughed as only Hindus can do. We crossed the
three miles of level plain under the torrid rays
of a sun which none but "globe-trotters" would
willingly have encountered. Thence, for fourteen
miles, it was steady "collar-work" over a road
heavy and sandy, in many parts, as the sea-shore.
And yet, neither rest nor refreshment did the
coolies take, further than a wash and a drink at
the occasional mountain rivulets which we crossed,
and a puff at an odd little hookah which they
handed round at intervals, one long whiff of which
seemed to impart fresh life to them.

Whilst daylight lasted the charm of the scenery
helped to carry us along without weariness.
Skirting, as we did for some miles, the base of
isolated Mount Abu, the black granite ramparts
of the Aravelli range rose from their bed of jungle
at the opposite side of the wide intervening plain,
which was fairly ablaze, like a prairie fire, with the
vermillion, flame-coloured blossom of the *tesu* or
palas-trees. After two hours we entered the pass,
hemmed in on either side by tangled jungle and
monstrous rocks fashioned into such strange, weird
shapes that one ceased to marvel at the native
propensity for peopling such formations with

spirits, sometimes good but mostly evil, for
Hindus are worshippers of nature in all its
moods.   Rajput horsemen overtook and cantered
briskly past us, and parties of pilgrims who had
been worshipping at Dilwarra piously greeted us
with "Ram, Ram," as we passed each other.   We
knew well that the steeps on either side of our
way were the home of wild creatures both savage
and otherwise, but all that we saw of such forest
denizens were companies of large, white-coated
apes that leapt from tree to tree above us and sat
solemnly munching their evening meal in blissful
unconsciousness that their own *raison d'être* might
probably be to become, on some ill-fated night,
the supper of some stealthy panther or hungry
young wolves.

Daylight merged into darkness in the swift
Eastern fashion which admits of little twilight,
and there were still three hours of journeying
before us.   The loneliness became oppressive as
we passed from one gorge to another—a tortuous
and winding way, and, in the darkness, like a
black, illimitable labyrinth.   The only sound which
broke the black stillness were the sharp cries of
the coolies to scare from the vicinity any wild
thing, from a panther to a carait,—a small and
deadly brown snake which infests these mountains,
—which might be out on a nocturnal forage.   And

the only gleams of light were from the embers of
occasional wayside fires left by pilgrims after
baking their *chupatties*, or by road-makers after
cooking their evening rice. At last a wild cheer
from the coolies, and the glimmering of many
lights behind a palm grove, obscured though they
were by the rocky ridges which rose now and
again between us and them, told us that Abu
was within measurable distance and our present
weariness well-nigh at an end.

Clearly the reward must be great which could
adequately compensate for a seven hours' journey
in a rickshaw so inhumanly contrived as was mine;
and as we sallied forth on the following day we
questioned with ourselves whether we had done
either wisely or well in being where we were at
such cost. Abu is a "hill-station" 7000 feet above
the plain, and the headquarters of the Rajputana
Administration. We walked for a mile or more
along the plateau upon which the cantonment
spreads itself in scattered buildings and bungalows.
Palms and acacias sprang from a rocky bed on
the right of our way, and a still higher ridge of
rock rose far above us on our left, from the summit
of which a small white temple peeped down upon
us. Up the steep heights, by a rock path, a long
line of pilgrims in single file wended their painful
way under the blazing afternoon sun to make

some simple offering at the shrine—perhaps a handful of Vishnu's white jasmine, which grows wild in the valley below, or it might be, a sprig of the sacred *tulsi* plant, the emblem of Parvati. Truly, in zeal these Hindus show us a rare and commendable example.

A sudden bend in the road, skirting a mound of granite which had been washed into undulations by the waters of primeval centuries, brought within range of our sight a group of simple, picturesque buildings—some clustering domes embowered in a grove of mango-trees and standing on a rock platform. The domes were supported on granite pillars, and their white *shunam* coating sparkled against the dark, rich green background of the mango foliage. But could these, indeed, be the world-famed Jaina temples of Dilwarra, of which it has been said by " one who knows " that " for minute delicacy of carving and beauty of detail they stand unrivalled even in this land of patient and lavish labour."[1] The group is formed of four or five temples enclosed by a wall which is sombred by centuries, and there is little externally to lead you to suppose that there lies within, one of the most perfect architectural gems in the world.

To reach the enclosure we had to pass through a narrow lane of squalid huts, crowded with

[1] Fergusson, *History of Architecture.*

solemn-looking men and women and hilarious children. At the entrance two Sepoys were stationed. A *peon* too was there, to whom we presented the order without which no European is allowed to enter. Then the door—a mere temporary barricade — was opened, and there was disclosed to us a treasure-house of art which made us silent with admiration and astonishment. Almost one could have knelt, like Pagans, and worshipped, or at least venerated, this thing of wondrous beauty, human creative power, and superabundant, life-long labour. For, paradoxical though it may seem, surely patient labour must ever accompany any great creative work of man's. One is the divine, the other the human element in it. Before the exceeding loveliness of Dilwarra's temples one sits feeling helpless and diminished, and searching for words forcible and vivid enough in which to speak of their beauty.

To the right, on entering the enclosure, an ascent of a few steps leads you into the first of the two principal temples. It is more modern by nearly two centuries, and more lavish in its ornament than the other, but similar in plan, and, as history has it, was built at the cost of two wealthy merchant brothers. The portico, which is the distinctive feature of the Jaina temples, as the gate-pyramid, or *gopura*, is of the Dravidian, here consists of a central dome, clustered around which are other smaller domes, the whole supported on forty-eight detached pillars. The sanctuary—a cell raised on a platform—occupies the further end, and over it rises the pyramidal spire which indicates the throne of the deity. In the cell is enshrined the god of dedication, Parswanatha, one of the greatest of the Jaina Tirthankars, or saints. The whole is enclosed in a courtyard measuring 140 feet by 90 feet, and round it runs a domed and double cloister which is raised some three feet above the level of the courtyard. The claustral pillars form the porticoes of fifty-five small cells or chapels which are recessed in the walls, and in each of which sits a fac-simile image of the cross-legged deity of the temple. This multiplicity of the same image is another characteristic of Jainaism. This is all of milk-white marble, and to attempt to describe the central dome, its supporting pillars with their bracket capitals, its friezes of classic beauty, its pedestals, its statues, and, above all, its pendant; or to do adequate justice in words, even, to the half-hidden recesses of the smaller claustral domes and of each separate pillar and entrance to the chapels, would be an impossible task.

We are told that this temple, small as it is, cost

the two brothers twenty million of rupees, and
that its building occupied fourteen years. But
granted the time and the money, how was this
great artistic work, in all its sumptuous grace,
realised? because it may undoubtedly be pronounced the finest example of architectural
carving in the known world, in spite of a certain
grotesquery in the sculpturing of the figures
common to all Hindu work. Could the result
have been achieved in some such fashion as
this? Granted the master-mind who conceived
the scheme, and suppose that he called to his aid
the most renowned sculptors of his style, and
placed in the hands of each a pillar, a panel, or
a dome,—which, by the way, are all executed in
single blocks,—with such instructions as these:
"Time and money are of no moment. Subject
to the general design, you are free to fashion
these marbles into the most varied and elaborate
sculptures. There shall be no repetition of
ornament, there shall be no plain surfaces,
and the work shall be finished in the highest
degree of perfection; and, although of the
utmost delicacy, it shall be so undercut and
relieved as to sparkle like the work of a silver-
smith."

And it is a fact that, although from the base of
the columns to the crown of the cupolas there is

hardly a square inch which is not carved with the
semblance of figures, niches, or foliage, yet there is
no confusion of detail, and the whole stands out
with a distinctness and brilliancy impossible to
realise without being seen. You have the utmost
profusion without vulgarity, a result so difficult of
achievement; and the whole scheme of ornament
is on such harmonious lines that the eye feels no
fatigue from its exuberance. On the contrary, it
only suggests, so true is it that all the arts are
kindred, a well-conceived and graceful symphony
or an exquisite idyll full of life and poetry. A
stream of architectural thought and purpose runs
through it all and adds to it another charm, that of
mystery; for, as Mr. Fergusson points out, " The
oldest Jaina monument may be of the tenth
century (those on Mount Abu belong to the
eleventh and thirteenth), but the style, when we
encounter it, is complete and full-grown. There
is no hesitation about the design, no wooden
clumsiness about the details. The whole is the
result of centuries of experience in stone architecture; but when and where we do not know."

The Jains, a Hindu sect who claim for their own
form of worship an antiquity of origin even more
remote than that of Brahmanism, come in great
numbers from distant parts of India, as well as
from their own special provinces of Guzerat and

A DOME IN DILWARRA.

Mysore, to worship at this, one of their holiest
shrines. Their religion has been spoken of as
"Buddhism without its asceticism," in other words,
without its monasticism. But as that formed the
very element and essence of Sakya Sinha's discipline, the comparison is hardly a felicitous one.
With its pantheon of twenty-four Tirthankars or
gods,—the last of whom, Mahavira, was the acknowledged friend and preceptor of the Buddha,—and
its mass of superstition and idolatry, the analogy
is much closer between the Jaina religion and the
Hinduism, from whence it sprang, than between it
and *Indian* Buddhism, which, from the time of its
birth until its utter extinction, aimed at the puri-
fying and reforming of ancient Brahmanism. All
three cling tenaciously to the doctrine of metempsychosis, and the Jains hold that no woman can
gain eternal happiness *as* a woman. She must
first so live as to merit re-incarnation as a man,
when she may have the opportunity of earning, by
another well-spent life upon earth, the privilege of .
entering into the company of the gods. The spirit
of the "advanced woman" has not yet reached
Jaina land.

A provident and paternal government has taken
under its guardianship these monuments of ancient
art. The poorer among pilgrims were in the
habit not only of " putting up" within the temple

enclosure, but of making fires and cooking their rice on the marble pavements, and were gradually laying waste the beautiful place. So the powers that be decreed, in the cause of art, that these things must not be, and, with much tact and discretion, ruled that no visitor should go there except at stated times, and he be furnished with an order from the Government agency; furthermore, that a fitting demeanour of reverence for the character of the place should be insisted on by the removal of hats or shoes; and that, though worshippers were free to go at all times, an authorised curator from among their own people should always be in attendance, who should be held responsible to Government for any further desecration of the temple's beauty. These laws are now in operation, and the incomparable Jaina temples of Dilwarra may therefore be handed down to the generations of countless centuries to come—truly a miracle of art and worthy of a pilgrimage.

BALCONY IN AHMEDABAD.

XIV.

THE NUREMBERG OF INDIA.

IT is a matter of no small wonderment that Ahmedabad, the ancient capital of the Guzerati Sultans and stronghold of the northern Jains, should receive so little notice from those travellers who come "o'er land and sea" avowedly to study the rare and exquisite art of the great Empire. Ahmedabad is at once the Birmingham and Manchester, the Nuremberg and Frankfort of India, all rolled into one prosperous, dirty, artistic city, the school and paradise of students in wood-carving, and the home of an unkempt, untidy-looking Guzerati population numbering one hundred and forty thousand. From the time of its foundation, when the fifteenth century was young, its vicissitudes have been many and great; and for the third time it has risen, phœnix-like, a still living and enduring monument of Hindu-Jaina art in its most characteristic purity. For the artisans and labourers of Ahmedabad dwell in houses, one panel

or one bracket of which, one would gladly carry
home at the cost of its own weight in rupees to
show England what can be and what has been
done in wood-carving; and there are streets of
such houses, and miles of such streets. When it is
a question of selection for purposes of sketching
or photography, one feels absolutely swamped in
quantities of good and desirable things, and it is
hard to know where to begin and when to stop.
The cornices and friezes, the pillars supporting the
upper projecting storeys, the brackets, the jambs
of the doors, and often the doors themselves, are
covered with carving so delicate, so relieved, and
so clean, that it might have been cut yesterday,
though the hands that fashioned it have been dead
for centuries.

From all time it would appear to have been a
necessity of the Hindu nature to beautify their
surroundings, and in Ahmedabad, though a subject
race, they have worthily fulfilled their traditions
by expending measureless labour and boundless
loving patience over the decoration of their
dwellings, the timbers of which they have covered
with fanciful and floriated traceries, diapers, and
niche-work which would make Adam Krafft himself hold his breath in wonder; for there is nothing,
even in the early work of Germany and Belgium,
to surpass it.

The endless variety of geometrical designs evolved by the iconoclastic Mohammedans, who would tolerate no semblance of living thing in their art, are in strong contrast to the flowers, foliage, birds, and beasts, conventionalised and interwoven, of the nature-worshipping Hindus; and both are to be found in their most perfect form in Ahmedabad, where the Moslem usurpers of the land of Guzerat had to subordinate their forms and ornament to the higher art of the people whom they had conquered, and to leave to them the beautifying of the city which, in the fifteenth century, they set about rearing. The Jaina temples, which they delapidated and despoiled, were turned to the purpose of constructing their own mosques. The roof of the Jumma Musjid, one of the most beautiful mosques in India, is supported on two hundred and sixty pillars, not one of which was ever wrought by Moslem hand nor meant to enrich Mohammedan mosque, but which were plundered and pillaged from the countless temples and shrines which the conquering Saracenic race considered it their mission to ravage and abolish. At the threshold of the main entrance, under the principal and most beautiful archway,—and here the arch is inserted as a distinctive religious symbol,—there is a large slab of black marble embedded in the pavement, the base of a Jaina

14

idol which was sunk, head downwards, on this spot, in that the faithful might continuously tread it underfoot.

One thing which Mohammedanism has *not* succeeded in treading out is the artistic genius and native architecture of the Jains. And this no one will deny who sees the Temple of Hutti Sing, which has been completed only within the last fifty years. Pass by the Delhi gate beyond the city walls, and there you shall find in this dignified pile an example of the purest and most excellent Jaina style, and which, "whether looked at from its courts or from the outside, possesses variety without confusion, and an appropriateness of every part to the purpose for which it was intended."[1] Neither has their fervour waxed cold, if it may be gauged by the sordid test of money; for this temple was the work of one man, who spent over it one million of rupees.

The mosques of Ahmedabad are countless, and among them that of Queen Sipri is pre-eminently beautiful. For the sake of its poetry and romance one would desire to believe the pretty story which tells how Ahmedabad owed its very being to the "dark loveliness" of the daughter of Assa, the Bheil chieftain whose dwelling was near the shores of the Sabarmati river; and how that the great

---

[1] Fergusson, *History of Architecture.*

Sultan had chosen that vicinity for the site of his princely city in order to be near her. But history is stern and facts are hard, and both go to prove that Sipri was Ahmed's daughter-in-law and not his wife. Be that, however, as it may, Sipri's little mosque is the most beautiful thing in this beautiful city. And mosque though it be, with its domes and its terraced and bracketed minarets, there is no suggestion of the Saracenic arch in the 'whole building, but "every part is such as only a Hindu queen could order, and only Hindu artists could carve."[1] Whether she ever worshipped in it is another thing, for though these aborigines of India profess a form of Hinduism, their religion is really a gloomy fanaticism and devil-worship which holds its adherents in an extraordinary thraldom, and it is hardly likely that the daughter of a Bheil chieftain, sultana though she was, would ever bring herself to kneel in a Mohammedan mosque.

India is, *par excellence*, the country and home of birds. They possess the land and multiply, and the diversity of their kinds is legion, from the high-caste pea-fowl of Rajputana to the homely sparrow and pariah crow of Bombay. In many Indian cities the birds are daily cared for, and fed more religiously than are the poor of our people

[1] Fergusson, *History of Architecture.*

at home, and in no place had we seen them so daintily housed as in Ahmedabad. Nearly every street has its own pagoda-shaped birds' *house*— not *cage*,—raised from the ground on pillars to the height of a lamp-post and beautified with delicately-wrought carving of exquisite design. To these homes of refuge the feathered folk of Ahmedabad resort for shelter and to feed and drink from the stores which are daily supplied to them at the expense of the city merchants. They are the relics of the ancient Jaina supremacy, and its successors of the present day have inherited both its traditions and its tender reverence for nature in a sufficient degree to perpetuate this beautiful old custom.

To photograph or sketch in the beautiful purlieus of Ahmedabad demanded some cool resolution; for no sooner was the camera planted than a concourse of eager, interested people gathered about us stopping the traffic, and, courteous, gentle, and anxious to help as they were, very effectually impeding operations. The inmates of the houses came out and looked with puzzled wonder, first at us and then at their own dwellings, to see what we could possibly find in the sometimes mouldering timbers to admire. The greatest pleasure we could afford them— such, at least, as were Hindus—was to put them

into the pictures, and that we were always ready
to do, though, as a race, they are not so pictorial
as the peoples of Southern India, nor even as the
Rajputs. They are fairer in colour, of a golden-
brown tone, and they look what they are, the
people of a manufacturing town; for the men of
Ahmedabad stand high among the handicraftsmen
of India. Their brocades are unsurpassed, their
metal work renowned, and their carving is a gift
of inheritance from the days of Anhulwara, the
city of their ancient magnificence, so rudely
wrested from them by the emissary of Toghluk II.,
the Tartar king of Delhi.

In the open spaces round about the city out-
skirts women may be seen winding cotton in a
primitive fashion into immense skeins for the
purpose of dyeing. The cotton is wound on an
enormous spool which spins round on a handle,
and this they hold aloft in the left hand whilst
with the right they guide the thread, by means of
a long forked wand, which bends like a fishing rod,
round four stakes that are driven into the ground
quadrangularly, about two yards apart. As they,
in the midst of the square thus formed, move
rapidly round from stake to stake, transferring to
them the cotton from the spool, the folds of their
saris, the curve of their limbs, and the flexuous
grace of their motion, have more of beauty in

them than any nautch that ever was danced before rajah, or daintiest measure that ever was trod on footboards.

Another sight which compels remembrance were the women in the corn-fields between Ahmedabad and Sirkej, where their garments made gorgeous splashes of Indian red or indigo blue amid the vivid, delicate green of the barley, and their brazen and silver anklets and bangles glinted and gleamed under the sunshine. Those same statuesque, queenly, bronze women may also be seen making bricks, watering roads, and even roofing houses. But on closer vision you find them uncomely of feature and labour-worn, and in many of their faces there is a look which tells plainly that the burden of their lives is almost greater than they can bear.

It would be an irony to designate as a *road* the track which leads through those fields to Sirkej. It resembles rather a dried-up, sandy river-bed, through which a carriage must plough and jolt its ways as best it may, the crowning grievance lying in the fact that there are two tolls to pay *en route*. The corn-fields and trees on either side of the way are peopled by monstrous monkeys with white whiskers, which, except for their black twining tails, twice as long as themselves, which hang like writhing snakes from the boughs upon

STREET SCENE, AMEDABAD.

which they squatted, very much resemble the old men among the neighbouring villagers, whose grain they pilfer and whose fruit-trees they rob, and who, out of deference to Hanuman, the monkey-god of war, would upon no account hinder, much less punish, their depredations.

Soon after leaving Ahmedabad by the city gate of Jamalpur, you cross the broad Sabarmati river—that is to say, it *will* be a broad river again after the rains. At present, in this month of March, it is so diminished and reduced as to transform its belt of rolling water into sundry channels which split and diverge and reunite, disclosing islets and borders of yellow sand. As we crossed by the bridge the river-bed beneath us was gay as a fancy fair, so thronged was it with *dhobies* and laundresses. The golden sands were charged with colour, both of that of the clothing that was drying and of the draperies of the women. Here, too, was solved the mystery of the lavish supply of fruits, vegetables, and sumptuous piles of melons to be found in Ahmedabad bazaar. For this same warm yellow sand is possessed of some life-giving properties, favourable, above all, to the growth of melons. Of these there is a rich, golden harvest in sun-trap beds which have been enclosed for their cultivation.

Two miles beyond the bridge, upon the left of

the road, there rises an ungainly domed building, traditionally pronounced to be the tomb of Azam and Mozam, the architects of Sirkej. If they designed it for themselves, their humility must have been profound; and if, as is more likely, they owe it to posterity, they have shared the common fate of great architects, and have been ill-requited, so far as popular recognition is concerned, for the impressively beautiful group of buildings, yet four miles farther on, which owes its being to them. Hindus they must unquestionably have been, for city of mosques and tombs though Sirkej be, there is no suggestion of an arch in the whole pile. The domes are supported on pillars with bracketed capitals of pure Hindu work, and throughout the entire buildings the style is another most interesting and curious example of the interweaving of Jaina art, exquisite in its grace, its poetry, and its finish, with the larger requirements, the nobler proportions and, in some sense, the greater breadth of the Mohammedans.

Mahomet Shah, "the Merciful," who in 1445 built the first tomb at Sirkej in honour of his father's friend, was, like the rest of the Saracenic builders of Ahmedabad, dependent on Hindu, or to speak exactly, on Jaina architects, for producing the group of tombs which, with their innumerable pillars and domed roofs, make up the city of the dead at Sirkej. Mahomet's Hindu queen, to whose father, the Rajah of Edur, he had restored his lost dominions, recompensed this act of magnanimous clemency by—with true Rajput facility—poisoning her spouse not many years after his succession. This, doubtless, accounts for there being no tomb at Sirkej in memory of its founder, whose career was thus cut short before he had accomplished this, one of the principal achievements in the lives of all princes of Tartar race.

Such is Sirkej, with its tombs and its mosques full of·ghosts and memories, and its tank full of alligators; a fact which, however, in no wise deterred the men and boys of the adjacent hamlet from risking their lives in the cause of *bakshish*, by diving from the heights of the terraces into the still black water which drowsed at their base. Neither did they shrink from the incidental rats which slipped, like shadows, in and out at the margin; nor yet from a snake which lay coiled, still and treacherous, on the sun-baked ledge. These, indeed, were the only indications of life in the sad and silent city. As we left the place, the black, nude figures standing motionless on the crest of the terrace walls, outlining themselves against the setting sun, were the last we saw of Sirkej.

How is it that India preserves the art of being
beautiful and graceful even in the midst of commerce and manufacture and money-getting, all
three of which are such potent causes in demeaning
and vulgarising the peoples of European nations,
even to the extent of decivilising them? The
" steam-fiend " reached Ahmedabad long ago. It
carries you to the city gate and roars and shrieks
in its factories. Industries flourish and trade guilds
abound. Yet the people remain what they always
were, full of simplicity, and with their sense of
beauty undulled and undiminished. Their life is
full of colour though their days are full of labour.
Go to the carpet factory in Ahmedabad, and you
shall find there nothing coarse, nothing squalid,
nothing paltry nor gross; only a number of open
sheds round a great quadrangle, in each of which
is set up an enormous carpet-frame. Behind each
frame squats a row of little boys making the
carpet—a very fine one of twelve stitches to the
square inch—whilst in front of it the pattern-reader
parades up and down calling out the number of
stitches and their colour, as though he were reading
a story to each small worker as he passes, and
receiving, as quick as thought, the answering "ay"
from the child-voices behind the upright frame
which screens him from them. The reader stopped,
and I peeped behind the frame to meet the gaze of

WINDOW IN SIDI SAID'S MOSQUE, AHMEDABAD.

a row of dark, serious, wondering eyes, looking out
of little bronze, Guzerati faces, upon each of which
a glimmering smile disclosed the inevitable milk-
white teeth. I doubt if the same number of English
fifth or sixth standard School Board children of a
similar class could be found capable of the same
ready apprehension and deft skill of finger.

In the same place men were carving in *shesham,*
or spurious ebony, and remodelling some of the
inimitable art of their own city. Models of the
two world-renowned windows of Sidi Said's
mosque, the traceries of each of which is formed
of one tree, the trunk and branches, the stems and
foliage conventionalised to the necessary purpose
and no further, were being carved for an American
lady who had had the taste to appreciate their
unobtrusive loveliness.

In this city of mosques and sculptured houses
it is not hard to find models for either pen or
chisel, and an artist in wood-carving might spend
months of study in the unique old place — for
unique it certainly is. And that constitutes one
of the marvels of India — that each of its cities
and art-treasuries has a stamp and character
peculiarly its own. Comparisons may be drawn
and analogies discovered. Relative causes and
effects may be traced; for race has subjugated
race, and one form of religion has dominated and

crushed another, thus producing a curious and interesting interweaving of styles. But gorgeous, barbaric Madura differs as widely from graceful, intellectual Dilwarra as do the superb red granite palaces of Delhi and Agra from the white, pearly beauty of Oodeypur or the coral - like city of Jeypore.

One might draw contrasts *ad infinitum*, and yet always find the characteristics and aspirations of the varied races who have peopled the great continent expressed in their work; finding thereby an object-lesson in studying the beauty of forms which we have never even dreamt of, and learning that architecture is, as Professor Fergusson tersely tells us, "as many-sided as human nature itself, and few are the feelings and aspirations of the human heart and brain that cannot be expressed by its means."

THE WALTER SCOTT PRESS, NEWCASTLE-ON-TYNE.

"The most attractive Birthday Book ever published."

Crown Quarto, in specially designed Cover, Cloth, Price 6s.
"*Wedding Present*" *Edition, in Silver Cloth, 7s. 6d., in Box. Also in Limp Morocco, in Box.*

An Entirely New Edition. Revised Throughout.

With Twelve Full-Page Portraits of Celebrated Musicians.

DEDICATED TO PADEREWSKI.

The Music of the Poets:
A MUSICIANS' BIRTHDAY BOOK.

COMPILED BY ELEONORE D'ESTERRE-KEELING.

This is an entirely new edition of this popular work. The size has been altered, the page having been made a little longer and narrower (9 × 6½ inches), thus allowing space for a larger number of autographs. The setting-up of the pages has also been improved, and a large number of names of composers, instrumentalists and singers, has been added to those which appeared in the previous edition. A special feature of the book consists in the reproduction in fac-simile of autographs, and autographic music, of living composers; among the many new autographs which have been added to the present edition being those of MM. Paderewski (to whom the book is dedicated), Mascagni, Eugen d'Albert, Sarasate, Hamish McCunn, and C. Hubert Parry. Merely as a volume of poetry about music, this book makes a charming anthology, the selections of verse extending from a period anterior to Chaucer to the present day.

Among the additional writers represented in the new edition are Alfred Austin, Arthur Christopher Benson, John Davidson, Norman Gale, Richard Le Gallienne, Nora Hopper, Jean Ingelow, George Meredith, Alice Meynell, Coventry Patmore, Mary Robinson, Francis Thompson, Dr. Todhunter, Katharine Tynan, William Watson, and W. B. Yeats. The new edition is illustrated with portraits of Handel, Beethoven, Bach, Gluck, Chopin, Wagner, Liszt, Rubinstein, and others. The compiler has taken the greatest pains to make the new edition of the work as complete as possible; and a new binding has been specially designed by an eminent artist.

LONDON: WALTER SCOTT, LTD., PATERNOSTER SQUARE.

THE SCOTT LIBRARY.

Crown 8vo, Cloth Elegant, Price 1s. 6d. per Volume.

ISSUE OF NEW VOLUMES.

Vasari's Lives of Italian Painters. Selected and Prefaced by HAVELOCK ELLIS.

"Vasari's Lives" may be approached for such knowledge as they afford concerning the history of art and the cataloguing of the art-products of the Italian Renaissance; or they may be approached for the light Vasari throws on the psychology of genius in artists, from which point of view he is incomparable. As the personal friend or acquaintance of some of the world's greatest artists, Vasari moved in an atmosphere of artistic tradition, which he has fully recorded. In this volume the editor has sought to gather from the voluminous *Lives* everything that is really of value regarding the intimate nature and habits of the great Florentine artists of the Italian Renaissance.

Laocoon; and other Prose Writings of Lessing. A New Translation, with an Introduction, by W. B. RÖNNFELDT.

This volume, representative of the prose of Lessing, contains, besides the Laocoon essay, those portions of Lessing's Dramatic Notes (*Hamburgische Dramaturgie*) which deal with various principles of dramatic art, and which are of permanent interest, together with the *Education of the Human Race*, Lessing's last contribution to theological discussion. A biographical note is prefixed to the introduction. An entirely new translation is here given.

Pelleas and Melisanda and The Sightless. Two Plays by Maurice Maeterlinck. Translated from the French by LAURENCE ALMA TADEMA.

The preface to this volume, while providing for the reader who is unacquainted with the peculiarly imaginative dramas of Maeterlinck an excellent introduction to them, furnishes also a bibliography of Maeterlinck's works. For the song in Act III. of Pelleas and Melisanda ("*Mes long cheveux descendent*"), the attempt at an adequate English rendition of which has baffled various translators, another song has, at the request of M. Maeterlinck, been substituted.

The Complete Angler of Walton and Cotton. Edited, with an Introduction, by CHARLES HILL DICK.

This is a carefully edited reprint of this famous book, prefixed by a biographical introduction. Pains has been taken in the selection of the type for this edition, which will be found one of the neatest and handiest of the many editions of *The Angler* which have appeared.

Lessing's "Nathan the Wise." Translated, with an Introduction, by Major-General PATRICK MAXWELL.

As the translator of Schiller's "Maid of Orleans," "William Tell," and of various plays and essays, General Maxwell's work has been received with considerable critical appreciation. An analysis of the play precedes the text in this volume, and copious elucidatory notes are appended. This translation of one of the most notable dramatic productions of the last century will be found as faithful and effective as any that has yet been given to the English reader.

LONDON: WALTER SCOTT, LTD., PATERNOSTER SQUARE.